MY JOURNEY

COL. KENNETH G. CASSELS
United States Army (Retired)

TO: MRS CHRIS BUTLER — IT WAS
NICE BEING WITH THE 1ST BN.
+ THE DINNER ON 23 AUGUST 2013.
RESPECTFULLY, Ken Cassels
08/12/2013

MY JOURNEY

Col. Kenneth G. Cassels, U.S. Army (Ret.)
Post Office Box 5579
Salt Springs, Florida 32134-5579
(352) 685-2148
kencassels@hotmail.com

MY JOURNEY is a true historical account that began in 1926 and continues to this day. All names, places and events have been reported and described as accurately as possible by the author.

To obtain a copy of this book or to have your book autographed, you may contact the author directly.

MY JOURNEY
Kenneth G. Cassels

Printed in the
United States of America
ISBN: 978-0-615-85899-9

First Printing 2013 by
E. O. Painter Printing Company, Inc.
DeLeon Springs, Florida

About the Author

Kenneth George Cassels' lifelong tour of duty began in a very small southern town in an era when each family knew its neighbors and looked out for each other. Children of all ages could wander freely without fear, a joy denied to the current generation.

Friendships made growing up were made for a lifetime, and his fond memories of his youth eventually called him back to that little town to become a great part of its history. When he retired from his civilian careers, he settled in Salt Springs, Florida, more a village than a town, where he currently lives with his wife of more than 55 years, Peggy.

Plant City, Florida, felt the tightening grip of the Great Depression when Ken was born, as did all of America. Perhaps his gratitude for the life he has had was sparked by his father being able to provide well for his family through very hard times as a result of having a good job.

From troubled economic times to World War II, a "conflict" in Korea, and then to the hell that was Vietnam, he steadfastly held on to the values instilled in him by his parents and to those he credits learning as a young boy in scouting, where he earned the rank of Eagle Scout. The values and leadership skills he was taught by the Boy Scouts of America were always a pivotal force in his life and remain so today.

As he grew from boyhood to manhood, he faced each challenge as it came his way with the spirit of a leader. At the still young age of 17, he volunteered for military service in the Army Air Corps Reserve and was called to active duty just before the end of World War II.

From that time and for the next three decades, his life's path seemed destined to be determined by his love of country and his innate desire to serve by exercising leadership in the profession that he ultimately chose. He achieved the rank of full Colonel in the United States Army during a career that over thirty-two years spanned the entire globe and the corridors of the Pentagon.

He saw combat in Vietnam, where he was thrown straight into the jaws of a formidable enemy and fought not just for his country, but for his life and the lives of those he led. In the late sixties, there were no "armchair generals" – those with rank served on the front lines alongside their men, and they fought and died with them. It was while leading his men in an engagement with an enemy force two to three times the size of his own that he was wounded. He and many of his men were awarded the Purple Heart for injuries received in that battle.

Their victory that day, in which they succeeded in repelling a well-trained enemy force against overwhelming odds, came at a cost which he is unable to forget.

Although he and the battalion of men he commanded realized success on the battlefields of Vietnam, he remembers not so much the victories but, instead, the courage and bravery he witnessed over and over again exhibited by the mostly young soldiers who, like himself, fought for duty, honor and country. It was by chance and providence that, unlike too many of those brave men, Colonel Cassels survived to tell his story.

After more than thirty-two years of service, Colonel Cassels retired from the Army and had two more satisfying careers in civilian life, one teaching exceptional students and one, lasting fourteen years, managing the nationally famous Strawberry Festival in Plant City.

Through it all, he kept the friendships made in childhood and the Army, finally retiring to a beautiful setting and a peaceful life in Salt Springs. Yet, even in retirement, he has found avenues of service and is doing so as this book is being written.

AN EAGLE SCOUT'S
RESPONSE TO WAR & PEACE

The Journey began at Plant City, Florida
24 December 1926

The Response Includes:

The Great Depression
World War II
Vietnam
Pentagon Duty
The All Volunteer Force
Support of National Guard & Reserves
First Retirement
Teaching "Special Needs" Kids
Managing Florida Strawberry Festival
Distinguished Member of the Regiment
Salt Springs Retirement
Honorary Colonel of the Regiment

Dedication

This book is dedicated to Peggy, my wife, and to my boys Kent and Scott. I had to leave them behind many times while serving my country. You and my country have been my life, and no words could ever be sufficient to express my love.

The part of my story recounting events in Vietnam is dedicated to the brave American soldiers who fight so fiercely and courageously for their country – both in wars of long ago and in current struggles for the cause of liberty. I know you fight for the ideals of freedom and for America and, when called upon, for the freedom of people in foreign lands.

Under extraordinary circumstances, you consistently demonstrate your unsurpassed courage, your patriotism, and your inherent values of *duty, honor, country*. You are the best military fighting force the world has ever seen.

To all the valiant American heroes who fight for their country, knowing that they might die, and to those they had to leave behind –

I salute you.

Kenneth George Cassels

The four cornerstones
of character on which the
structure of this nation
was built are

Initiative

Imagination

Individuality

Independence

Eddie Rickenbacker

Table of Contents

MY JOURNEY

Preface i

Acknowledgments iii

Permissions iv

Introduction v

Chapter 1 The Beginning 1

Chapter 2 Becoming an Eagle Scout 6

Chapter 3 Times of Change 10

Chapter 4 Active Duty 15

Chapter 5 Scott Field 20

Chapter 6 Commercial Fishing 23

Chapter 7 University of Florida 24

Chapter 8 Regular Army Officer 26

Chapter 9 Japan 28

Chapter 10 Company Commander 30

Chapter 11 Love and Marriage 33

Chapter 12 Fort Benning 38

Chapter 13 Army Language School 41

Chapter 14 Saudi Arabia 44

Chapter 15 82nd Airborne Division 47

Chapter 16 Command & General Staff College 49

Chapter 17 Hawaii (Commander-in-Chief Pacific) 50

                Prologue to War 50

                Vietnam on the Horizon 52

Chapter 18 Vietnam - Quan Loi 54

Chapter 19 Vietnam – Rome Plow Operation 61

Chapter 20 Vietnam – Fire Support Base Jim 69

Chapter 21 Vietnam – Operation Kentucky Cougar 74

                Battle of Binh Long Province 74

                10 August 1969 74

                12 August 1969 76

                5 September 1969 81

Chapter 22 The Big Red One 85

Chapter 23 The Pentagon 88
Chapter 24 Atlanta, Georgia 95
Chapter 25 Patrick Readiness Group 98
Chapter 26 Standing Down 105
Chapter 27 Medals and Awards 107
Chapter 28 Teaching School at Dover 109
Chapter 29 The Florida Strawberry Festival 115
Chapter 30 Transitions 137
Chapter 31 Life in Salt Springs 142
Chapter 32 The New Generation 155
Chapter 33 Bandido Charlie Tells How It Was 40 Years Ago ... 158
                   Captain Phillip Greenwell 159
                   First Sergeant Alfredo G. Herrera 165
                   Spc. Ron Mackedanz 172
                   Colonel Kenneth G. Cassels 176
Chapter 34 Honorary Colonel of the Regiment 179
Chapter 35 A Small Town Heritage 187
Chapter 36 A Matter of Honor 189
Epilogue 190
Medals Awarded After 43 Years 192
Appendix A Timeline 194
Appendix B Military Education 202
Glossary and Abbreviations 203
Index 207
Photographic Memories 220
Review 233

Preface

An autobiography includes the author's memories, both good and bad, his feelings, joys and sorrows and all the emotions in between, the expression of his core values, and the pivotal events of his life. Usually, the purpose is to leave a legacy for family and friends, but sometimes it also can give voice to those who may have been forgotten or who were silenced before their stories could be told.

Vietnam was a very long time ago, by anyone's timekeeping. A part of this story relates some of my experiences "in country" during a period which felt much longer than it was. If at times it appears to be a simple recitation of seemingly mundane events, please try to understand that brevity in the written word was the way I was trained to write during my military career. Words can tell the story, but victory comes from action.

Memories of events that happened then are still as vivid as though they happened yesterday. Dusting off those memories and bringing them to the surface of my mind has brought pain along with pride for the men with whom I served, for it was a time of war and I witnessed men wounded and killed. Those scenes are indelibly imprinted and cannot be erased.

Because of so many brave soldiers who fought valiantly against an enemy force of unbelievable odds, I survived Vietnam and continued to live my life surrounded by family and friends. In recording the part of my past dealing with Vietnam, I hope to honor those who came home but whose futures were affected by what happened, and I especially endeavor to honor those who did not come home.

Good fortune led me into rewarding careers after leaving military service, and I have led a life in retirement that I always dreamed of. Those parts of my life may not be filled with the drama that only a life-and-death struggle can present, but they are just as much a part of my history as the time I spent serving my country and, perhaps, provide proof that life does go on and it can be very good.

I am unashamed to "wave the flag" – life must be lived believing in ideals, and those of America are worthy of sacrifice. *Duty, honor, country* must never become meaningless words on paper or slogans mouthed by politicians using rhetoric to paint themselves patriotic and to justify continuation of their own agendas.

Many politicians and historians called what happened in Vietnam a "conflict," and they still argue to this day about why America was in Vietnam. But make no mistake; regardless of the reasons for being there given by those in political power or by the media and the historians, the soldiers who served did so because of a love of freedom and country, and it was indeed a war.

It was a war if you measure it

by the number of brave Americans and others who were willing to fight a war in a foreign land for the ideal of freedom

by the number of veterans who came home but could not forget, some suffering from physical wounds, others from emotional scars, and some from both

by the number of families who waited at home for their loved ones to return, so many of whom never did, and

by the outstanding heroism and courage of those who fought, and those who died.

This is my final tour. These are my memories.

Acknowledgments

This book would not have been written without the encouragement of my family and friends, because some of my memories were deliberately put away long ago.

I have thanked in person most of the people who assisted me with the project, but I now take the opportunity to gratefully express my thanks to all of the following individuals for allowing me to include stories of their experiences, to those who assisted me in reviewing drafts of the manuscript, and to those who gave me invaluable advice:

Al Herrera

Phillip Greenwell

Ron Mackedanz

The Bandido Charlie Association, 1/16th Infantry (Mechanized), 1st Infantry Division, and its members

Permissions

Permission for the use of the copyrighted material in this book has been received as follows.

The stories of Phillip Greenwell, Al Herrera and Ron Mackedanz as they appear in the chapter titled *"What was it like 40 years ago? Bandido Charlie Explains"* have been reprinted with permissions obtained from (1) the three men whose stories were told; (2) the Cantigny First Division Foundation, which published these stories in the *Bridgehead Sentinel*, the Summer 2008 newsletter of the Society of the First Infantry Division, in the article titled *"40 Years Ago: Vietnam 1969, 3 Bandido Charlie veterans remember the Battle of Binh Long Province"*; and (3) Ball State University, which interviewed Phillip Greenwell on August 2, 2008 and published written and videotaped transcripts on its website (Cantigny First Division Oral Histories No. V 269-13).

The article *"From Jungle Colonel to Festival General"* in the chapter *"Transitions"* has been reprinted in full with permission of the Tampa Chapter of the Military Officers' Association of America (formerly known as the Retired Officers Association, Inc.), which published the article in *The Retrospect*, Vol. 3, No. 3 (March 1997 pgs. 1 and 8), and has been reprinted, in part, by permission from the *Tampa Tribune*.

Photographs are either the personal property of the author, in the public domain, or used with permission from the owners or photographers. Most of the photographs depicting people and places in Plant City were obtained from the Plant City Photo Archives and History Center in Plant City, Florida. Attribution is noted and the photographs are presented in this book with my gratitude.

Introduction

A life cannot be summed up in only a few words, but major events and the places where those events occurred often can be recorded in a simple list. An attempt has been made to do so here.

The author's journey has taken him to many places where major events were lived, including:

Plant City, Florida
Wildwood, Florida
New Port Richey, Florida
Clemson College, South Carolina
Keesler Field, Mississippi
Scott Army Airfield, Illinois
Occupation Duty - Japan
University of Florida, Gainesville
Commissioned 2nd Lieutenant, Infantry
Teaching school in Starke, Florida
Fort Benning, Georgia (Infantry School)
Fort Jackson, South Carolina
Hokkaido, Japan (Company Commander)
Marriage to Peggy Sparkman, Plant City, Florida
University of Connecticut – ROTC Duty
Fort Benning, Georgia (both sons born here)
Army Language School, Fort Ord, California
Royal Saudi Arabian Airborne Duty, Saudi Arabia
82nd Airborne, Fort Bragg, North Carolina
Command & General Staff College, Ft. Leavenworth, KS
CINCPAC, Hawaii (including 6 assignments to Vietnam)
1st Infantry Division, 1st Brigade (Infantry)
Vietnam–Commander, 1st Inf. Battalion (Mech) (*leading the bravest of the brave as they attacked elements of the 9th North Vietnamese Army Division*)

Pentagon Duty, lived in Fairfax, Virginia
Atlanta, Georgia, Fort Gillem
Patrick Air Force Base, Patrick Readiness Group
(influencing National Guard & Reserve)
First retirement to Plant City, Florida
Teaching the "special needs" kids in Dover, Florida
General Manager, Strawberry Festival, Plant City, Florida
Second retirement to Salt Springs, Florida
Honorary Colonel of the Regiment (volunteer HCOR
duty), making trips to Fort Riley, Kansas

Life goes on, to be lived with honor and treasured until the last sunset, and so

the Journey continues …

C hapter 1
The Beginning

On December 24, 1926, a prominent medical physician, Dr. T. L. Maguire, went to 703 West Tever Street in Plant City, Florida, to deliver a baby. At 2:00 p.m., Kenneth George Cassels was born to Samuel G. and Alma Watson Cassels. Dr. Maguire accomplished the delivery, recorded the birth, and went back to his office. Treating patients at home in those days was a common practice.

My mother was a housewife devoted to raising her three children. She ultimately lived to the age of 96, and was still in good health until the year before she died. She outlived my father, a railroad conductor and part-time farmer, by many years. I was particularly close to my mother, who always had faith in me and encouraged me to be all that I was capable of being.

When I arrived in the world, I had two sisters, Marguerite, 10 years old, and Christine, 5 years old.

Soon after I was born, our family moved to 1105 West Terrace Drive, a 20-acre farm about four miles north of town.

The house on the farm didn't have electricity. It would have been truly unique if it had, because in that time and in that place electricity was a rare luxury.

Without electricity to run a pump, there was no running water, but we did have a good, two-inch well with an operative pitcher pump. The only "on" switch was a jar of water to prime the pump, and the only source of power was a pair of human hands to work the lever.

We didn't have a refrigerator, but there was an icebox, and twice a week ice was delivered by horse and wagon from the downtown ice plant.

Cooking was done on a kerosene stove. My mother was resourceful and a hard worker, and expertly utilized that now-antique curiosity so that no one in the family ever missed a good home-cooked meal.

All over the deep South, especially on rural farms, besides lacking electricity to bring running water inside the home, there was a lack of either the knowledge, availability, or means to install indoor plumbing. Bathrooms with flush commodes were still in the future for many homes. Instead, even in the middle of the night or the cold of winter, we went outside to visit the amenities provided by a two-hole outhouse. A nice hot shower was unavailable as well; we took our baths in a galvanized washtub filled with water heated on the kerosene stove.

After dark, lighting was provided by candles or by kerosene lamps.

Air conditioning, central heating and mosquito control were non-existent.

When you're born into a loving family and have all the essentials of life, you accept the way things are as if they have always been that way, and I accepted the way things were in my world. In those days, money did not determine whether you were rich or poor. How much you had in the bank or your material possessions did not reflect true wealth as we considered it to be. We knew very well that all of that kind of treasure could vanish in an instant. To us, wealth was measured by whether you were a member of a loving, happy family. We counted our riches by counting our blessings. I look back now and know that I was truly wealthy in what I had.

My memory isn't photographic, but it is quite good and goes all the way back to very early childhood. When I was about 3 years old, I remember overhearing someone say that the stock market had crashed and that the country was in for a severe depression. Of course, I had no idea what a "stock market" or a "crash" or a "depression" were, so it had little to no effect on my state of mind.

During the next few years, many people would be out of work. Our family was more fortunate than some, and our father's railroad job and part-time farming would be the key to our survival during the era of American history known as the Great Depression.

Remembering a Happy Time

When I was between 3 and 4 years old, our family went to the very first Strawberry Festival held in Plant City. The Plant City Lions Club is credited for starting the festival, which was sponsored as a civic event to celebrate the bountiful harvest of strawberries, a crop depended on by many of the local farmers.

I remember that everyone around me seemed to be quite carefree, smiling and laughing as they enjoyed the festival.

There was a carnival atmosphere, with a midway that had rides, booths and sideshows, and more food all in one place than I had ever seen before! It was a happy time for all.

The highlight of the day was the coronation of the festival's very first Strawberry Queen, a lovely young girl named Charlotte Rosenberg. I'll always remember the first festival, which lasted three or four days in March 1930.

Charlotte Rosenberg

Woodrow Wilson Elementary School

I started attending Woodrow Wilson Elementary School at five and a half years of age. My sisters and I, accompanied by other children in the neighborhood, all walked about a mile and a half to school. It was a fine walk, and the weather was always good. Most of the children walked to school barefooted, as few of the roads were paved and the soft sand felt good on bare feet.

Our family was blessed to have really good neighbors, including the Scotts who lived next door. Harry and Ora Scott had two children who were my age. There was a barbed-wire fence between our house and the Scotts' house. Once, when climbing over that fence on the way to play with the Scott children, I got caught in it. I was unable to get free from the barbs in the wire that had caught on my clothes, so I yelled as loud as I could for help. Thankfully, Mrs. Scott heard the shouting and came running to help me out of my predicament.

Other neighbors at the farm included the Wallers, the Wrights, the Fuells, the Clarks, and the Hurons.

Temporary Move to Tampa

My father's railroad job required him to go wherever his assignment was. It took us to Tampa, Florida when I was in the third grade, and the farm was left behind.

It turned out to be a temporary relocation. When I was in fourth grade, our family returned to live in Plant City in a house at 909 West Tever Street, just a short distance west of the home where I had been born.

This house had been refurbished, and besides the three bedrooms, living room, dining room, and kitchen, it had a bathroom with a commode, lavatory, tub, and shower with hot running water – all made possible by electricity! It included a block of property with an orange grove.

We lived in this house throughout the time I attended the fifth and sixth grades at Woodrow Wilson Elementary School.

Miami Relocation

Then once again, my father's railroad job took us away from Plant City for a short time, about eleven months, to Miami, Florida.

There, when I was 11 years old, I had my first real paying job with the Curtis Publishing Company selling magazines door-to-door, magazines such as the *Ladies Home Journal*, *Saturday Evening Post* and *Liberty*. In season, I sold mangoes, a tropical fruit.

Bonuses were paid in the form of model airplanes that I happily constructed from the kits. The enjoyment this provided may have been a factor in my developing an interest in aviation.

Our address, I still remember, was 1022 S.W. 11th Street. It was just a few blocks from 8th Avenue, one of the busiest streets in southwest Miami. That intersection is now known as "Little Havana." At that intersection, for just a nickel, I would take the bus to downtown Miami. There, I would sell all of my magazines in just a few minutes. At 11 or 12 years old, that was quite an accomplishment. This area of Miami is now heavily populated by Cubans seeking the American dream. Castro was never mentioned when I lived there.

The time in Miami seemed to pass by quickly, and my father's job once more took us back to Plant City.

Overture to Scouting

Mike Sansone was an immigrant from Italy who cut my hair when we returned to Plant City. While cutting my hair, he would tell me about working with Troop 5 of the Boy Scouts of America. He told me that Troop 5 had more Eagle Scouts than any other troop in the United States. Troop 5 and Troop 4 are competitive troops in Plant City.

Today, Mike is honored and remembered in Plant City by a park named for him, Sansone Park. He was a person I greatly admired.

Chapter 2
Becoming an Eagle Scout

It was in the seventh grade when, at 12 years of age, I became extremely interested in the Boy Scouts.

The Boy Scouts taught me first and foremost to memorize and understand the scout motto: *"Be Prepared."* Besides becoming familiar with the motto, I also learned the scout law, which has twelve points. A scout is:

1. Trustworthy
2. Loyal
3. Helpful
4. Friendly
5. Courteous
6. Kind
7. Obedient
8. Cheerful
9. Thrifty
10. Brave
11. Clean
12. Reverent

I also memorized the scout oath:

> *On my honor, I will do my best to do my duty to God and my country, and to obey the Scout law; to help other people at all times; to keep myself physically strong, mentally awake, and morally straight.*

There are six ranks in scouting: Tenderfoot, Second Class, First Class, Star, Life, and Eagle Scout. Earning merit badges took a lot of work and earned for me the rank of Life Scout.

Mary L. Tomlin Junior High School was the name of the junior high school that I attended in Plant City, and it was there that I learned to play the saxophone and became a member of the school band.

It was during this period that I developed very close friends. Wilbur Hicks lived three blocks away on Sanders Street, and Wilbur's dad, Dr. Hicks, was the Scoutmaster. Dr. Hicks came to our home to suggest to my mother that Wilbur and I be allowed to go to a Boy Scout camp for two weeks for scout training. This was a big thing in those days, as money was still tight because of the ongoing depression. Nevertheless, my mother agreed, and my intense interest in scouting developed even further.

The camp was northwest of Tampa and there, the scouts learned canoeing, swimming, lifesaving techniques, nature appreciation, and other skills. Associating with so many others and learning to get along with them was just as meaningful a skill as others I learned at camp.

The closest neighbors, at 1007 North Ferrell Street, were the Smiths. Mr. Smith owned a car sales agency in Plant City, and his wife was the English teacher at Tomlin Junior High. They had two sons, Mac and Patrick. Both boys were just a little younger than I was.

One of Mac's Christmas presents one year was a pair of boxing gloves, and during the next couple of years we just about beat each other to death with them – in a somewhat friendly way, of course! Mac later also became very involved in the Boy Scouts.

Other neighbors included the Tuckers, the Winns, the Harrels, the Wallers, the Broogemans, the Ergles, and the Don Waldens. Don's dad, from time to time, was the city mayor.

During the seventh and eighth grades, my circle of friends expanded, and their homes stretched closer to downtown Plant City. They included the Nuckols, the Blains, the Ramsdells, the Morgans, the Parkers, and the Spanns.

The Morgans had rather unique names. The father was "Rat" Morgan, also a mayor of Plant City at one time. "Sucky" was the mother, "DoDo" was the daughter, and "Panky" was the youngest. Who could ever forget them with names like that? Mrs. Morgan always made the kids feel at home in her house. Her daughters' friends were always welcome.

Buddy Blain's mother invited me to their house on several occasions, and both Mrs. Blain and Mrs. Nuckols were especially good to me. As a Star Scout, I examined and approved Buddy and C. B. on their Tenderfoot tests.

Wildwood and the Court of Review for Eagle Scout

Then once more, after the eighth grade, my father's job took our family away from Plant City, this time to Wildwood, Florida. At the time, Wildwood had a very large railroad yard.

Wildwood did not have a scouting program but, after what seemed to me to be a very long time, a good friend became the Scoutmaster and I was able to complete all the requirements for the rank of Eagle Scout.

I temporarily returned to Plant City for the Court of Review for 25 merit badges and the Court of Honor. There, the promotion to the rank of Eagle Scout was made final and witnessed by the Plant City Boy Scouts.

I consider this to be one of the highlights of my life.

**Eagle Scout
Pocket Patch
1933-1955**

**Boy Scout Handbook
cover in 1927**

**Eagle Scout Badge
& Patch today**

Centennial Badge

Chapter 3
Times of Change

My memories of Wildwood are quite fond, as there were many of our relatives living there. Our grandmother, Ollie Watson, lived there, and she made the best sweet tea ever.

Our mother was the oldest of nine children born to George and Olivet Watson. She had two sisters, Pearl, who married a man named Shelton, and Jewell, who became Mrs. Barrett. One sister died at birth. Her five brothers were Clyde, Roy, Allen, Hoyt and Maxie, all of whom married. I was very good friends with Clyde Watson, one of Aunt Ruth's children.

During this time, I grew very close to my mother, who always showed me that she had faith in me and encouraged me to be all that I was capable of being.

I was also close to my father, even though his work for the railroad kept him busy and took him on trips away from home many times. On several occasions, he was the conductor on the Orange Blossom Special that ran between New York and Miami. He rode it from Wildwood to Miami, and again on the return trip from Miami to Wildwood. It was exciting when I got to meet him at the railroad station. On one trip, I got to go with him on the round trip to Miami and back, a very special memory to me. Many people know that the Orange Blossom Special has been immortalized in American country music.

While in Wildwood during the ninth and tenth grades, I played saxophone in the high school band. After school and on Saturdays, I found a job at the Sell Rite Grocery Store. There was only one manager, so grocery orders called in to the store had to be delivered, a job which fell to me. By this time, I had procured a valid driver's license.

Marguerite and Christine

It was during this period in my life that my two sisters were moving on in their individual careers.

Marguerite completed twelfth grade at Plant City High School in 1934 and enrolled in Florida Southern College in Lakeland, Florida the same year. She completed courses for a teaching degree in education in 1938, after which she taught high school for two years in Webster, a very small farming town not too distant from Wildwood. She then transferred to teach at a high school in New Port Richey on Florida's west coast not far from Tampa. There, she met and married Fred K. Marchman, also a high school teacher.

Christine completed high school at Plant City High in 1939. She then pursued a college level degree in business at a school in Tampa for two years, after which she worked as a teletype operator and office manager in Tallahassee, Florida.

Christine met and married Robert (Bob) C. Zimmerman, a lieutenant in the Army Air Corps. Bob was a pilot who flew P-40s and later P-51 fighter planes, and also flew for the famous "Flying Tigers" under the guidance of General Claire Lee Chennault in China.

Flying Tigers lined up on a Chinese airfield
It is believed that no planes survive today except as wreckage
These were the P-40 type aircraft flown by
Robert Zimmerman (1st Lt.) WWII 1943-44

Change and Loss

When I was in the tenth grade of high school, it seemed that the whole world changed.

On the 7th of December 1941, Pearl Harbor in Hawaii was bombed by the Japanese. According to our president, it was "*a day that will live in infamy.*" The United States was now at war with the Japanese and the Germans, and later with the Italians who had decided to enter the war on the side of Hitler and the Third Reich.

Later that month, my sister Marguerite and her husband Fred invited the family to their house in New Port Richey. While there, we learned that our father had extremely high blood pressure which had already affected his kidneys. The diagnosis: terminal Bright's disease. Although the diagnosis could not predict how long he had left to live, I believe my father realized he would not last long and that the end was near. He died in New Port Richey a few short months later on March 31, 1942. Our father's sister, Mrs. Clifford Ergle, and her family hosted the eulogy and burial in Plant City.

After the funeral, I went back to Wildwood and stayed with Grandmother Ollie until the end of the school year.

New Port Richey

Because of the United States' entry into the war, Fred was given a direct Army commission. Before he reported for duty, which would last for the duration of World War II, he made arrangements for a large house in downtown New Port Richey. Marguerite took me and our mother into her new home, where we lived for the next two years.

These two years turned out to be very interesting and were a period of personal growth for me. Because the able-bodied men were rapidly being called to service in the armed forces, volunteers at home were needed "to take the place of" those who enlisted or who were drafted, so I always had a job of some kind – one of which was being a volunteer fireman, where I became experienced in driving a fire engine (always a boy's dream!).

Other jobs included being a "soda jerk," driving trucks, and clerking in a grocery store. While working at the grocery store, I also gained experience delivering groceries in town and driving a Model "A" Ford to and from Tampa to pick up produce. In one job, I pumped gasoline and changed oil and filters.

During season, I picked oranges and grapefruit for processing. Using the long wooden ladders to get to the fruit was fairly daunting, as there were no helping hands at the bottom holding the ladder to keep it from toppling; if you fell off or the ladder slid away from the tree, it was sometimes a long way to the ground. The citrus packing plant at Elfers, Florida, presented another opportunity for employment, and my *Tampa Tribune* bicycle paper route required getting started at 4:30 a.m.

To do my duty to God and my country included joining the Methodist Church in New Port Richey.

The Graduating Class of 1944

The 1944 graduating class at Gulf High School was a hard-working group of dedicated students. They all knew they had to keep their community going while the country was at war, and they had to do their part for the war effort. There were only 13 students in the class, 9 girls and 4 boys:

Johnny Decubelis	Henri Ellen Norfleet
Thomas Jefferson Frayne	Lily Zo Conner
Kenneth G. Cassels	Viola Walters
Jerald Herndon	Marie Lysik
Lois Dingman	Jackelyn Draft
Azalee Herndon	Azalee Townsend
Imogene Balcom	

There were many other friends in the school, and a few will be singled out.

Dale and Eddy Swartsel were very good friends. Dale was the quarterback on the Gulf High football team.

"Honeymoon" Island

On one occasion, Dale and I were invited to sail from New Port Richey to Honeymoon Island near Clearwater on a boat that Jeff Frayne had designed and constructed.

Not fully realizing what could be in store for us, we decided to spend the night on the island. As twilight fell, masses of mosquitoes also descended – but it was too late and too dark to board the boat and evade them. As you can imagine, we could hardly wait to sail home at daybreak the next morning and escape the hordes of stinging, high-whining pests!

At full daylight, when we could see better, we discovered that every inch of our exposed skin bore the marks of those mosquito bites.

C hapter 4
Active Duty

On 28 July 1944 at 17 years of age, I was sworn into the Army Air Corps as an Enlisted Reserve (ACER) at MacDill Army Airfield in Tampa, Florida.

The physical examinations by the Army doctors at MacDill were extensive. Fortunately, I passed the examinations and was declared eligible to attend pilot training — that is, except for one thing — I was just 17 years old and one must be at least 18. Accordingly, it was their decision for me to take college courses and military training at Clemson College, a military school specializing in the field of engineering.

Though not on active duty, reserve training was scheduled for me until I reached 18 years of age. The regimentation of military training pleased me and seemed to fit until I could be accepted for flight training.

The attack on Pearl Harbor convinced President Franklin Delano Roosevelt that we must enter the war against Germany, Japan, and Italy. This all happened while I was in the tenth grade. On 6 June 1944 the United States and its allies launched *Operation Overlord* against a force led by Hitler. President Roosevelt was beginning his fourth term as president.

On 12 April 1945, President Roosevelt died at Warm Springs, Georgia. Two days later, I stood in a formation consisting of all Clemson College students, paying our respect and admiration to a leader who had guided the nation through the Great Depression and now had provided direction for the war effort. It was an honor to be at the Clemson train station and salute as the steam locomotive passed by carrying the president's body from Warm Springs to Washington, D.C.

Lesson in Reality

While at Clemson, I developed pneumonia and was transported to the nearest Army base where hospital treatment was administered. This base was near Greenville, South Carolina, just a short distance from Clemson.

During the time I was there undergoing treatment, I saw soldiers wounded in the *Battle of the Bulge* in Europe who were placed in the same hospital. Seeing these men and their injuries brought the war home to me as a vivid reality, and I learned much of what war was all about. I felt that perhaps, even though as a 17 year old I had volunteered for service, I had not understood fully that my commitment would involve personal combat and sacrifice, but I saw first hand how huge a price these wounded men had paid in fighting for freedom.

Leading Flight 1

Little did I realize that the training at Clemson would "fit like a glove" for my next assignment on active duty. The close-order drills, physical training, calisthenics, distance runs, and constant inspections would prove to be extremely worthwhile for future assignments. Nor did I foresee that the leadership skills I learned during training would be tested quite soon.

Upon completion of coursework at Clemson in June 1945, I was inducted into active military duty. The Army then sent me to Keesler Airfield at Biloxi, Mississippi for Air Corps basic training.

Something occurred on the first day I lined up alongside the other students, an event that undoubtedly changed the path my career in the military would take.

The officer in charge asked the group, "How many of you men are Eagle Scouts?" Niles Jester from Tampa, Florida and I raised our hands. Then the officer addressed the two of us and said, "Ok, gentlemen, you two will take charge of Flight No. 1 and Flight No. 2." (A "flight" in the Air Corps is equal to a platoon in the Army, about 40 men.)

Continuing, he said to me, "You, Cassels, you will be responsible for all that Flight No. 1 does or fails to do. You will move the flight from point 'A' to point 'B.' We of the Air Corps will provide instructors at each point for your basic training."

Did that new assignment inject fear? Was I scared? On both counts, the answer was "Yes!" Did I have the courage to accept the challenge to lead and the determination to do well with this much responsibility? You bet I had the courage, and I was determined.

The courage was there, perhaps because of the training I had received as a Boy Scout and in the military school at Clemson College. Perhaps it was there because I had been taught to *go first, to lead the way, to provide a way, to be the chief, to give direction, to set an example, to act as a guide.* And perhaps it came from my desire to become a leader in spite of my fear.

I had learned a great lesson from Eddie Rickenbacker, a pilot who fought in World War I and became an American hero. Rickenbacker said *"Courage is doing what you are afraid to do."* He also said that *"There can be no courage unless you are scared."* Rickenbacker's courage was exemplified when his B-17 bomber ran out of fuel over the Pacific and crashed in the ocean. He and six others existed on a life raft for 24 days before being rescued.

Leading Flight 1 through basic training proved to be quite challenging for me, but I discovered that I also enjoyed it. Basic training in the Army Air Corps was the same as the Army infantry training; the instructors taught us to shoot, move, and communicate. As it turned out, because the war was winding down in Europe, pilots were plentiful, so training to become a pilot was not a possibility for me.

World War II ended when President Harry S. Truman declared victory in Europe (VE Day) to be May 8, 1945. However, our president knew that the war was not over in the

Pacific and that if it became necessary to invade Japan, the American and Allied losses would be great.

Soon after meeting with Stalin and Churchill, President Truman learned that American scientists had succeeded in developing what would become known as the "atomic" bomb. He gave the order for two of these bombs to be dropped on Japan in the hope that it would end the war so that America and the Allies would not be required to invade Japan.

On 6 August 1945, Hiroshima was hit by an atomic bomb delivered by the *Enola Gay*, a B-29 bomber. History tells us that it was devastating. Three days went by, and the Japanese had not surrendered. On 9 August 1945, a second atomic bomb was dropped on Nagasaki, Japan. That did it; within days the Japanese emperor announced the surrender of Japan, followed by a formal signing of an unconditional surrender aboard the battleship *USS Missouri* on 2 September 1945.

When the surrender was announced, I was at Scott Army Airfield in Illinois. Personnel on the base went wild with elation as the news spread that World War II was finally over. St. Louis, Missouri was our destination to celebrate.

My disappointment in not being able to fly airplanes quickly disappeared as I realized that my own life and the lives of countless other Americans and their allies could have been forfeited in the fighting if we had been forced to invade Japan.

After a day of celebration in St. Louis, the KP ("kitchen police") assignment or the schooling would be welcomed. It was clear to me that going on with the cryptographic schooling was a must, and I accepted the fact that my orders to the Far East would result in occupation duty in Japan.

For peace of mind in the face of that unknown, I relied on my scout oath — *to do my duty to God and my country, and to obey the scout law* — and believed that all my training and schooling would enable me to live up to the scout motto, *"Be Prepared."*

**Ken G. Cassels
United States Air Corps
A World War II Veteran**

C hapter 5
Scott Field

The next assignment was at Scott Army Airfield in Illinois, where I was to learn to be a cryptographer. The base was near St. Louis, Missouri. At some point in years past, my sister Marguerite had taught me to type and I had developed a speed of about 30 words per minute. This skill came in handy during training.

The job would involve handling classified material, so the Army proceeded to perform a background investigation on me. While those security checks were being done, I pulled KP for 28 days straight. At the end of that time, I could quickly and efficiently break eggs with both hands and serve breakfast to airmen hurrying through the food line. This duty began each morning at 4:00 a.m.

The top secret security clearance was finally received and after completion of training as a cryptographer, I received orders for the Pacific Far East Command.

Because the war had ended when Japan surrendered in August 1945, the new orders were to serve in Japan as part of the occupation forces. I was sent on a troop train and spent several days en route to Phoenix, Arizona for staging and processing, then continued by train to the port of embarkation in Portland, Oregon. Everyone boarded a troop ship and sailed down the Columbia River to the Pacific Ocean.

For 18 days I was the forward latrine orderly and *seasick* for the entire voyage!

On arrival at Yokohama, Japan, it was snowing and bitterly cold. We traveled by railroad cars to our next stop, Irumagawa, Japan. That city, like Yokohama, was mostly destroyed. Trucks took us the rest of the way to Showa, Japan, an old Japanese military base, where I would work as a cryptographer. I served in Showa for a full year.

During the time I was in Japan, Wilbur Hicks and I had dinner in Tokyo and talked about the days we were Boy Scouts in Plant City. I also met Jeff Frayne in Tokyo. Reminiscing with Jeff brought back memories of all the jobs we had held in New Port Richey and graduating from Gulf High School, and especially our memorable adventure to Honeymoon Island.

At Showa, there were several of us who were trained as cryptographers and in the use of the teletype machines. The lines of communication between 5th Air Force headquarters in Tokyo were always kept open 24 hours a day. We accomplished the main mission, but still found time on our hands and wanted to see more of Japan. We were not restricted as to where we went and took advantage of the rail system, which was always on time and very efficient.

Since the emperor of Japan had declared a complete surrender to the U.S. forces, we felt safe anywhere we went.

The most impressive thing we observed was that the Japanese people were the hardest working people we had ever seen. Their ability to engage in agriculture in a country that was very small geographically was incredible. Rice and other food products were being grown on the sides of mountains, and it appeared as if they could make water run uphill for the rice crop.

Several of us climbed Mount Fuji, which is over 12,000 feet high. We took two jeeps to Gotemba, which was as high as our vehicles could go. The rest of the trip was the climb to the top. At the summit, the crater was three miles across, and the view from there was breathtaking. Such a beautiful sight nature had made!

We made several trips to Tokyo, where we visited the Supreme Headquarters and observed General McArthur, Supreme Commander for the Allied forces, assigned to Japan. His behavior and normal routine not only signified his personal courage, but demonstrated a phenomenon I had already observed as I traveled throughout Japan. The general and his wife had a driver but no other security presence — in spite of the fact that he would have made a prime target for anyone seeking revenge. Because of the acceptance of defeat by the people of Japan and their diligent efforts to move forward to rebuild their lives, the general and his wife felt secure. This simple fact was another sign that the long war was truly over.

It was evident that the Japanese people were working hard to rebuild their country. Of course, the United States helped them in this effort. During the decades following the war, Japan would once again become an industrial nation that would become at one point in time second to none.

My tour in Japan was interesting and enjoyable, but most of all I developed a good feeling about the people of Japan. One could not help but feel that these people, our former enemies, were now sincerely intent on being our friends.

After serving the year, we were sent home by troop ship, which took 14 days. This time, the seas were calm and I found it much more enjoyable, not having to deal so much with sea sickness.

I was honorably discharged from the Army on 15 December 1946. After discharge, I stayed in the reserve force for seven more years.

C hapter 6
Commercial Fishing

After returning from WWII service as a corporal in the Army Air Corps, it was time to look for a new job. I found employment with my brother-in-law, Robert Zimmerman, who was working as a commercial fisherman based in Tarpon Springs, Florida.

The fishing boat was 42 feet long, had 500 feet of mainsail, a much smaller jib, and a gasoline-powered engine. We could sometimes receive transmissions from the WFLA radio station and get the weather reports we needed before heading out into the Gulf of Mexico. We went out on the Gulf about 50 miles offshore where the depth was about 22 fathoms, fishing deep for grouper. If we couldn't fill the large ice chest with grouper, we moved on to deeper water for red snapper.

The job was dangerous, as the waves at that depth were high and communication was limited to receiving weather updates. Our trips in the Gulf normally lasted three to four days.

Working with Bob was a real pleasure. His war stories about WWII and serving as a pilot of P-40/P-51 type aircraft in the China and Burma theaters of operation made things interesting when the weather was bad enough to prevent fishing.

Three or four months of this plus an unsuccessful 16-day fishing trip to the Camphee Banks of Mexico led Bob and me to the conclusion that there must be a better way of making a living. For that reason, we both found productive work with Desmond Little, a general contractor in New Port Richey.

By this time, my brother-in-law Fred Marchman had also returned from WWII service and was teaching mathematics at Gulf High School in New Port Richey. My sister Marguerite continued teaching at Gulf High.

C hapter 7
University of Florida

Desmond Little provided several months of employment and exposure to the house contracting business. As interesting and enjoyable as it was, it occurred to me that since the WWII GI Bill provided an opportunity and the means of gaining a college education, I should take advantage of what I had earned.

Dale and Eddy Swartsel, friends in New Port Richey I had played football with at Gulf High School, encouraged me to make this bold move. They even suggested that I join their fraternity. I was appreciative of the offer and my friends' encouragement.

Encouragement also came from Buddy Blain, C.B. Nuckols, and Wilbur Hicks from Plant City. I had passed Buddy and C.B. on their Tenderfoot tests in the Boy Scouts. All three were Eagle Scouts and now were veterans of WWII. They also suggested that I join their fraternity. An invitation to live with Buddy, C.B. and Wilbur in an apartment on University Avenue in Gainesville, Florida, was gratefully accepted.

I entered the University of Florida as a freshman and joined the Kappa Alpha fraternity, where I became house manager. This earned me a welcome salary of $50 per month. Even with the extra income, however, sometime between the junior and senior years of college the money that made attendance possible would run out. Another source of income had to be found. I learned that the Army was paying $27 per month for Infantry Reserve Officer Training Corps (ROTC) students, so I volunteered for that job, too.

The ROTC students were sent to Fort Benning, Georgia for training. While there in 1950, between my junior and senior years of college, the Korean War began. In spite of the advent of war, our group was not called up but returned to school in Gainesville where we were commissioned Second Lieutenants of Infantry in June 1951.

I didn't graduate from the university until August 1951. At that time, reserve officers were not being rushed into service in Korea, so I accepted an offer to teach at Bradford County High School. Mr. Bill Scruggs, the professor I had interned under, may have influenced my acceptance for the position by Mr. Partin, principal of the school. Mr. Partin understood that a call-up was a probability, and the teaching contract he offered me was contingent upon my not volunteering for active duty before the one-year contract was completed. I agreed to that condition.

The second scout law, to be *loyal*, must be honored.

C hapter 8
Regular Army Officer

Only a few days after going to work at Bradford County High, I received a letter from the Department of the Army. The letter read, in part,

> You were designated a Distinguished Military Student when commissioned. Now that you graduated in August from the University, we are designating you as a Distinguished Military Graduate. Due to your demonstrated outstanding leadership, we are offering you a regular Army commission.

I responded to the letter, saying that it was an honor to be rated so highly by my fellow students, but advising that I had made a commitment to a school principal who had employed me on the condition that I would not volunteer for service until the one-year contract was completed. I thanked the Army for the offer but rejected it.

Several days passed and, much to my surprise, I received another letter from the Department of the Army. In part, it read,

> Dear Lieutenant: We respect an officer who honors his commitments. Our offer for you to become a regular Army officer stands valid. Accordingly, we request you go to a senior officer there in Starke, Florida, where he will swear you into the regular Army. When you are sworn in, we will place you on active duty without pay and allowances. When your principal is satisfied that you have completed your contract, then report to Fort Benning, Georgia for further training.

The active duty regular Army commitment was effective September 25, 1951. This meant that I had made a four-year commitment to serve in the Army before being eligible to resign, and my long-term service would be as an Army officer.

After I completed my teaching contract, I reported to Fort Benning for more training, and then it was on to Fort Jackson in South Carolina to teach those just coming into the service.

In what seemed like no time at all, it was time to go to Korea to take my turn at leading troops. I was confident I could be a good leader and accomplish any mission assigned to me.

Peggy Ann Sparkman

It was understood that most combat infantry officers serve eleven months of combat duty before being returned to the states, so a delay in going to Korea was granted for me to put my personal affairs in order before I was required to report to the port of embarkation.

When I returned to Florida from Fort Benning, I heard about a convention being held in Tampa by the Florida Education Association. There was enough time for me to go, so I decided to attend. While at the convention, I met one of my college roommates. Wilbur Hicks invited me to go with him to Bradenton, Florida and meet someone he described as a beautiful girl from Plant City who was currently teaching school in Sarasota, a town near Bradenton.

I remember that meeting well. Peggy Sparkman was a pleasure to be with, and for three days we enjoyed each other's company. Neither of us made any commitments; we both thought that after my eleven months of combat service in Korea, I would return.

On to Korea. There was a boat trip to Yokohama again, but this time the seas were calm.

Chapter 9
Japan

A big surprise greeted us at Yokohama – the boatload was split. Half were sent directly to Korea and the other half to Hokkaido to retrain the First Cavalry Division before it would be recommitted to combat duty in Korea. My bunkmate on the ship was part of the half that was sent directly to combat in Korea. He was killed on his third day in country.

Hokkaido, the northernmost island in Japan, gets very cold; 48 inches of snow overnight is common. It was a world far distant, in more ways than one, from home.

I was assigned as a platoon leader in Love Company, and we were sent to the field right away to take part in a brigade exercise that would be observed by "umpires." My platoon was designated as the aggressor. A platoon usually has about 40 people, and for this exercise it also had three tanks assigned.

A map reconnaissance revealed that there was one piece of high ground that might be employed to enable us to block the advance of the main body. I moved the infantry and tanks to this high ground under cover of darkness. The tanks were placed in hull defilade, and the infantry was well dug in.

The advancing force was made aware of our position, but because of the advantage my platoon gained by its position on high ground, the umpires assessed many casualties to the opposing force.

The success of my taking the high ground was made known even at battalion level. The scout motto is "being prepared" — and my men were prepared to be at the right place at the right time. Some called it outstanding leadership.

Author Ken Cassels with his mother,
Alma Watson Cassels
Ken was on his way to occupation
duty in Japan 1944-46

C hapter 10
Company Commander

It wasn't long before I had a new job.

I was transferred to be the new commander of King Company. Being a company commander as a second lieutenant was not expected, but I welcomed the responsibility and the chance to lead a larger body of men.

I had always been a student of history, which taught me that the 1st Cavalry Division was one of the combat units deployed on the Yalu River in northern Korea when Chinese forces entered the war with the North Koreans. That division took heavy casualties, partly because of a dearth of proper clothing, footwear and a lack of training on fighting in extremely cold weather.

The deployment of King Company to Hokkaido, which had conditions similar to those the troops would be expected to endure in Korea, would provide better winter training for them. This was to be done under the guidance, in part, of Maj. Kavoric from the Army of Finland, who was an expert on cold weather warfare.

Training would concentrate on proper footwear, clothing, and specialized equipment. During winter months, equipment and training included skis, snow shoes, thermal boots, and achios (snow sleds) to carry machine guns, mortars, explosives, fuel, heaters and tents.

The mission of the infantry is to close with the enemy by means of fire; to maneuver in order to defeat or capture him; or to repel his assault by fire, close combat, and counterattack. The troops in King Company were taught to shoot, move, and communicate in spite of the extreme weather conditions. We trained to be prepared.

During the summer months, the company moved to firing ranges, usually near Chitose, where unit training concentrated on weapons. The company officers included:

2nd Lt. Ruben O. Figuero, an ROTC officer from Puerto Rico, was the XO of the company and also our ski instructor. To prepare for that assignment, he had completed a two-week course to learn skiing.

2nd Lt. DiSerafino, also an ROTC officer, was leader of the 1st Platoon.

2nd Lt. Winfield Holt was a West Point officer who led the 2nd Platoon.

The other platoons in the company were led by senior non-commissioned officers (NCOs).

Promotion to First Lieutenant

My promotion to the rank of First Lieutenant came on March 25, 1953.

After a year of training in Hokkaido, the unit was trained and ready for deployment to Korea. However, the war ceased with the signing of a truce, so the First Cavalry Division moved south to the vicinity of Tokyo to continue training and to stay prepared for any future mission.

My assignment as King Company commander changed, and I became the S-1 (Adjutant) of the battalion of the First Cavalry Division.

8th Cavalry Division, Hokkaido, Japan
training before returning to Korea
pictured left to right:
2nd Lt. Ken Cassels, Company Commander
2nd Lt. Winfield Holt
2nd Lt. DiSerafino, Platoon Leader
2nd Lt. Ruben O. Figuero, Co. Executive Officer

C hapter 11
Love and Marriage

After some 28 months in Japan, new orders would send me stateside and into service with the University of Connecticut at Waterbury, Connecticut as an ROTC instructor.

Upon reassignment, I was planning to take a 30-day leave for a Florida vacation, but the Professor of Military Science and Tactics had other plans. He told me that I was to be operational at Waterbury ten days from the date of arrival, so my vacation was considerably shortened.

When I arrived in Florida, Peggy and I renewed the relationship that had started 28 months earlier. After a brief courtship, we agreed to marry as soon as practicable.

Getting Married

The date we first considered was in December, but the First United Methodist Church in Plant City was not available then, so the ceremony was moved back.

The magic date was November 20, 1955.

I returned to duty and made arrangements to buy a house in Watertown, Connecticut near the assigned duty station at Waterbury. In Plant City, Peggy made arrangements for the wedding. November 20 was going to be a wonderful day!

Peggy did not seem like a new member of the military family, as she and I had corresponded during the 28 months we had been separated. I also had consulted with Peggy on September 25, 1954 when my four years of regular Army commissioned service were completed. That was the date I was first eligible to resign my commission and return to civilian life. Though not binding, she did not object to my decision to continue service in the Army and make it my career.

Peggy sent out invitations to the wedding and selected her attendants: matron of honor Mary Evelyn Whitehead; maid of honor Patricia Chapman; and bridesmaids Dotty Pollock and Margaret Sikes.

I chose my best man, 1st Lt. Billy T. Davies, and groomsmen Wilbur L. Hicks, Jr., Lester "Buddy" Blain, Jr., C. B. Nuckols, Jr., David Walden, and Dale Swartsel. Peggy's dad, Amos L. Sparkman, gave her away.

Honored guests were Peggy's mother, my mother and my two sisters Marguerite and Christine, their husbands Fred and Bob, and Peggy's brother Perry Sparkman and his wife Virginia. The reception was held at the Methodist Church in Plant City.

Peggy in her wedding dress

Peggy's brother, Perry Lamar Sparkman, had returned to Plant City after WWII was over. He had been trained by the Army Air Corps to be a belly-gunner and/or radio operator on a B-17, a 4-engine bomber. He had flown 28 missions over Germany before the war ended. After obtaining a degree in agriculture from the University of Florida, he was employed by the Chevron Oil Company and was in charge of the "Ortho" portion of that company in Florida and Cuba. Perry and Virginia had made a good start on a family by this time.

The Honeymoon and a New Car

After the wedding, Peggy and I went to stay at a hotel on the beach on Florida's west coast for two nights. Airplane tickets to Detroit, Michigan had been arranged for earlier, and we boarded the plane at Tampa.

This was Peggy's first flight on a four-engine reciprocating engine type aircraft. She was wide awake all night, watching the blue flame coming from the engines' exhaust!

Upon arrival at Detroit, we went to the factory and picked up a new Pontiac hardtop that I had contracted for while still in Japan. It was a beautiful blue and white automobile, but ran only 18 miles after leaving the factory. That was just the beginning of problems with the Pontiac.

We continued to Niagara Falls on our honeymoon. The falls were beautiful, but to Southerners like us it was very cold. When we finally left Buffalo, New York, it was during a blizzard — the first time Peggy had ever seen snow.

It was then the car started overheating, and we found out that the thermostat was stuck. It took two more days in Buffalo to get the car repaired before we could travel on to Waterbury.

We stayed with my realtor until the house I had purchased was finished. The house was in Watertown, several miles from Waterbury where the branch of the university was located. It was on a high hill, which was easy to negotiate except when ice and snow prohibited us from driving the Pontiac uphill. When that happened, we parked at the bottom and walked up.

Settling In and Southern Ingenuity

The Professor of Military Science and Tactics in Storrs, Connecticut, came to visit the school in Waterbury where I was teaching. I invited the colonel, who was my boss, to meet my bride at our home in Watertown, and the colonel accepted the invitation.

When we moved in, all we had was a stove, refrigerator, and a double bed. Peggy served coffee on two orange crates which functioned as a table and chair. The sugar bowl was made of aluminum foil, and the cups which held the heated instant coffee were Styrofoam. I believe the colonel felt sorry for us; he later sent Peggy an electric frying pan for a housewarming gift.

Peggy learned quickly that clothes hung out during Connecticut winters would not dry, but instead would freeze. She also learned that a wringer type washing machine would not automatically cut off as soon as the proper amount of water was reached. If the water supply was not cut off when the tub was full, the overrun went downstairs into the basement.

At Christmas we went home to Plant City for visits and to pick up our wedding gifts, welcome additions to our meager household basics: eating utensils, pots and dishes. The car made it to Plant City and back to Waterbury without incident.

The University of Connecticut

The new assignment at the University of Connecticut branch at Waterbury was interesting to both the assigned non-commissioned officer and to me. The NCO took care of weapons training and close order drill and was also in charge of the drill team. I taught military history. As a southern lieutenant, my final exam question was:

"Who won the war of Yankee aggression?"

Of course, all the students failed this final question. It was without prejudice, however, since I didn't count it in their final scores! They all passed the exam.

Peggy and I were asked to chaperone freshmen and sophomore parties, possibly because we were both young at heart. We did enjoy the task, but learning to stay erect on ice skates wasn't easy!

Kent Lamar Cassels

After a wonderful, blissful year and a half, we learned that Peggy was pregnant. Kent Lamar Cassels was born in Columbus, Georgia on August 21, 1957, and I took several days off to celebrate our first child. Peggy's mother and dad also came to see their first grandson and to help Peggy with this added responsibility. Everyone thoroughly enjoyed the reunion. My mother was able to come and visit us later at Fort Benning

Once I had finished two years at the college, I was allowed to transfer to Fort Benning. The transfer was completed before the advanced career course started in September, so I worked in the "Training Aids Department" until the course began.

C hapter 12
Fort Benning, Georgia

Fort Benning, Georgia is the Army post charged with providing education and training for leaders of the infantry. A great deal of intensive study accompanies the advanced course. Many demonstrations of various weapons are conducted in the field throughout training.

Paratrooper

When I had completed the advanced course, I volunteered to be trained as an Army paratrooper. This course lasted only three weeks, but it presented a huge challenge because it was potentially dangerous. On one jump, I broke a bone in my ankle. After that incident, Peggy would always tell me, "Land on your *head*, Ken, and you won't get hurt!"

Surprisingly, I found that I actually enjoyed the training, but successfully completing the course required me to demonstrate a certain degree of courage – after all, why should anyone *want* to jump out of a perfectly good airplane? But I could now wear the "Paratrooper" badge on my uniform.

Pathfinder

Next came the Pathfinder course, which taught me to provide navigational assistance to Army aircraft. Selecting landing areas and drop zones – perhaps behind enemy lines and under the cover of darkness – required a lot of dedication and intensive training. I found this course to be quite demanding, although this test of my ability was rather enjoyable as well. I could now wear the "Pathfinder" badge on my uniform.

Army Ranger

The next, and toughest step so far, was volunteering to take further leadership training as an Army Ranger. At 32 years of age, it was hard for me both physically and mentally.

In training from time to time, students were denied sleep and food. The theory was that if the leaders-in-training could still lead after being denied enough sleep and sufficient food, they could pass on to their soldiers what they learned from the exercise: that even while enduring such hardships, you could accomplish much, much more than you thought possible.

The course at Ranger's School lasted about six weeks, including two weeks of rigorous physical training which also involved hand-to-hand combat. The next two weeks were at Dahlonega, Georgia for the mountain phase, then two weeks in the Yellow River at Eglin Air Force Base in Florida. This last phase was the hardest, as we stayed wet most of the time and were sent on very long patrols with little food or sleep.

After successful completion of Ranger School, I was authorized to wear the "Ranger" tab on my uniform.

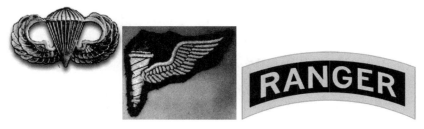

Captain

All of my efforts were rewarded by my promotion to the rank of Captain on October 25, 1958.

My captain's rank qualified Peggy and me to be eligible for larger and better on-post quarters, which made it possible to have visitors come and even stay at our house. Peggy and I both wanted to remain at Fort Benning, since our second child was on the way.

Scott George Cassels

Scott George Cassels was born on 26 January 1960, at Tripler Army Hospital at Fort Benning – a happy day! Again, Peggy's mother and dad came to help celebrate our growing family, and my mother also was able to visit us occasionally at Fort Benning.

Assignment to the Ranger Department

My request to be assigned to the Ranger Department at Fort Benning was approved. My job in the department was to teach the students offensive and defensive tactics.

My first task in this assignment was to pass the two-week instructor's training course and qualify as a platform instructor, representing the commanding general at the Infantry School. Using impeccable English and good thought patterns in teaching was a must.

At the time, I was one of only a few qualified Rangers teaching the offensive and defensive tactics course at the Ranger Department at Fort Benning. Because of this, from time to time I was tasked to be a "lane grader" at Dahlonega for West Pointers attempting to qualify as Rangers. These cadets and the other students were learning the basic principles of leadership.

A New Adventure

The time spent at Fort Benning was a very pleasurable period for me, Peggy, Kent and Scott, but in 1960 it came time to move on to the next assignment. This new assignment would take us clear across country and prove to be quite a challenge, not only for me but for Peggy as well. We would be moving from the east coast of the United States and the Atlantic Ocean all the way to the west coast and the Pacific.

A new adventure was ahead, but in spite of the coming challenges I knew that my duty to God and my country would be upheld. I would remain a good scout.

Chapter 13
Army Language School

The new assignment was at the language training school in Monterey, California.

The old Pontiac was on its last leg, so it was time to buy a new automobile. Peggy and I went to a small Ford dealership in Americus, Georgia and purchased a new six-cylinder, four-door Ford Falcon station wagon. It had only three speeds forward, and the new car was Ford's cheapest. It didn't even have air conditioning, but it suited our pocketbook and it was dependable enough to take our family to Monterey.

Without air conditioning, it was particularly trying for Peggy to take care of two children in the back seat, one still nursing, when we crossed the desert. After this experience, she understood to some extent how pioneer women making the long trek across the desert in wagons must have felt.

We made it to Monterey, but had to rent an apartment for a while because quarters at Fort Ord were not available when we arrived. When quarters became available, we moved on base.

Fort Ord

Fort Ord was established in 1917 as a maneuver area and field artillery target range for the Army. It was one of the most attractive locations of any U.S. Army post, because it was close to beaches and was blessed with great weather. At the time we were posted there, it also had a language training school.

At Fort Ord, Peggy experienced an occasional earthquake, and she spent part of each day searching for Kent and Scott, who were playing in the dense Pacific fog that rolled in every morning. On the weekends, we took the boys for outings along the seven-mile run adjacent to the Pacific Ocean.

The fairly small post quarters we lived in tested Peggy's resourcefulness and fortitude in keeping Kent and Scott quiet while I was occupied in memorizing portions of the Arabic language. This task took several hours, five nights a week. Spending that amount of time was required because we were tested on a daily basis on the subject material we learned the night before.

The encroachment into my time with my family detracted quite a lot from any enjoyment I might have otherwise taken in learning a new skill at the language school. Friday night, Saturday and part of Sunday was the only family time we had.

My Language Instructors

I soon discovered that all of my Arabic instructors were from Baghdad, Iraq, which I found a little strange because I knew that my next assignment was going to be in Saudi Arabia. Even though the Saudi dialect is *similar* to that spoken in Iraq, why wouldn't our teachers be brought to the school from Saudi Arabia instead of Iraq? I still don't know.

The two countries' basic religion was the same, however; the majority of the people were of the Muslim faith. I learned from our instructors that Mohammed studied the teachings of Christ before he founded the Muslim religion, and that he recognized Christ as a prophet but not as the Son of God. All of this information was to be learned as part of the required memorization in the Arabic language.

Getting Ready for Separation

Fort Ord was a nice place to live. Toward the end of the one-year school, it was time to plan for the year I was going to spend in Saudi Arabia.

Peggy and the boys wanted to live in the Plant City area while I was gone. Her mother and dad added a large room to their house as well as an extra bathroom so Peggy and the boys could live there. Both of her parents looked forward to having Peggy and the boys stay with them while I was away.

Although it was my chosen career, the thought of separation from my family for a full year was heartbreaking and tough for all of us.

In getting ready for the trip from Fort Ord to Florida, Kent and I constructed a carrier to fit on top of the car to make extra space for luggage, and it worked quite well. In addition to Peggy and the boys and me, my mother, who was visiting at the time, would be traveling back with us. There would be a total of five people in the Ford.

My mother went on to New Port Richey, and Peggy and the boys stayed with Mom and Dad Sparkman in their home in Dover, Florida, a small town just "next door" to Plant City.

Kent and Scott enjoyed the country living, black dirt, and riding the tractor with Granddaddy. Everyone enjoyed going to Sunday school at the Methodist Church, where they met many friends.

It was there that I met my former scoutmaster, Dr. Wilbur Hicks, Sr. It was once again a meeting at the First United Methodist Church, where he was also a member. Being a scout under his leadership was always an honor.

Chapter 14
Saudi Arabia

Once the family was settled in Dover, I traveled on to Washington, D.C., to attend a ten-day course at the State Department. Instruction there focused on diplomacy in Arabia, because the mission was far more on how to be diplomatic than on teaching the Saudi Arabian airborne battalion something about training as a military force.

On to Saudi Arabia.

The first layover en route was Portugal, where the wine was so good that it took three days to repair the ailing four-engine Convair. The next stop was overnight in Madrid, Spain, where the french onion soup was the best ever. The Spanish people were memorably courteous and hospitable. The next stop was in Libya, where I saw a four-engine B-24 bomber that had been left there from WWII. History recorded several B-24 bombing missions from Libya to Europe.

This stop was the first time I was able to talk to native Arabs in their own Arabic language. They could understand everything I said, and I could understand *most* of what they said. There was a one-night layover there, and it was then on to Saudi Arabia.

I landed at Dhahran in Saudi Arabia, a large airport next to the Persian Gulf. The U.S. Army Air Corps boys met me there and flew me to the duty station across the peninsula at Jidda, a port on the Red Sea. At that time, the American Embassy was also located at Jidda, as were most of the other foreign embassies. All of the embassies in Jidda were eventually moved to the capital at Riyadh. The American military compound where I would be staying was situated between the U.S. embassy and the Saudi airborne battalion base. The staff at the American Embassy always welcomed personnel from the American compound.

In Jidda, I was greeted by a friend from the Army Language School, Capt. Joe Wilson. Joe was a career officer and had been in Saudi Arabia for about ten months. He and I were now only two Army soldiers in a sea of U.S. Air Force officers assigned to train Saudi airmen.

The next day Joe took me to meet Lt. Col. Ruzzi of the Saudi army. The colonel was the commander of the Royal Saudi Arabian Airborne Battalion, and spoke perfect English.

That same day, Joe and I visited the parachute packing facility. These parachute riggers were professional in every way. The battalion jumped without a reserve chute, in spite of which they never had a malfunction – *incredible.*

The battalion was made up mostly of Arabs from the many Bedouin tribes in Arabia. They were tough as nails, as the unit had been engaged mostly in physical training for several months before my arrival. They hadn't been able to jump, however, because their C-123 type aircraft had been in Italy being repaired during that time.

The repaired C-123s were returned from Italy after I had worked with the battalion for about two months. Joe Wilson was transferred to the 101st Airborne Division at Fort Campbell about the same time the C-123s arrived, so I was left alone as the sole Army representative living with the U.S. Air Force.

Occasionally, the battalion would perform parachute jumps in the desert. When they did, they were sometimes witnessed by King Saud, the Saudi Arabian ruler. The king sat in an overstuffed chair placed on a large Persian rug, along with some members of the royal family. Several bodyguards accompanied the king. When the paratroopers completed their demonstration, many expensive watches were given to them as gifts.

Since my role as an adviser wasn't very demanding, I spent some time with Air Force friends at the "Creek" (a part of the Red Sea). We became quite proficient as scuba divers, and on one occasion I went down with an Air Force friend to a depth of 150 feet. We saw a large white shark when we reached that depth. In hindsight, of course, making that excursion was *dumb.*

During Ramadan, a Muslim religious holiday that lasts about two weeks, I hitchhiked on Air Force aircraft back to the USA. Visiting with the family for six days was fantastic. I had been away from the boys for so long, I had to try very hard to convince them I was okay and that I would return when my assignment was completed. Peggy's dad was a big help in this respect, as he had served during WWI in France and had returned. He was also a hunter, and each night he would gather the boys around him and tell them hunting and fishing stories. They still remember some of those stories.

Sometime after my return to Saudi Arabia from this trip, the Army chaplain there took about ten Army personnel from all over the country to the Holy Land for a four-day tour. We were allowed to visit anywhere we wanted except Israel. Jerusalem was a divided city. As it happened, the King of Jordan was visiting Jerusalem and we were privileged to talk to him. He was very impressive and spoke perfect English.

It was on this visit to the Holy Land that I filled a bottle of water from the River Jordan, which was later used in the christenings of Kent and Scott at the Methodist Church back home.

Because of its importance to our way of life, I wanted to learn more about the oil industry, and I learned that the Arabian American Oil Company (Aramco) and other oil companies had been in Saudi Arabia since about 1933 looking for oil, which was first discovered at Jebel Dhahran near the Persian Gulf in 1938. Aramco was well respected by both the Saudis and the USA.

During the time I spent there, I spoke the Arabic language some in Arabia and in Jordan. Hopefully, the effort I had made to learn Arabic was worth it to the State Department and the Arabs; in my time there, I discovered many Arabs could speak English.

My assignment was finished after one year, and I received orders to go to the 82nd Airborne Division at Fort Bragg, North Carolina.

C hapter 15
82nd Airborne Division

Leaving Saudi Arabia, I went straight to Plant City. The 82nd had assured me that post quarters would be available, so we relaxed for 30 days before I reported for duty at Fort Bragg. Then we shipped the stuff in storage to Fort Bragg, and it wasn't long before I was reporting to the G-1 (Adjutant) of the division.

Assignment to the G-3 (Operations) Section took me to the third floor of the division. There, an armed guard checked my credentials and summoned the Contingency Plans Officer with the rank of major. That officer welcomed me in and said he had been expecting me. He introduced me to an intelligence officer with the rank of captain. The typist for the group was a corporal who was very intelligent and personable.

From that day forward I was "let out of the cage" for some exercise and occasionally to board an Army helicopter to make qualifying jumps-for-pay, which added $110 per month for Peggy. She was always encouraging me, saying "Jump, Ken, *jump!*"

The job in the Contingency Plans Area was to develop strategic and operational plans for various parts of the world. Even though plans are developed, authority for the execution of those operational plans is held only at the highest level of government.

It must be obvious that I was now working full time in a classified area. Classified information is *that information which must be protected in the interests of national security.* Only those with a need to know and the proper security clearances are given access to classified material. Peggy did not know what I did at the division and never asked.

Peggy and I enjoyed many fine friends who also worked at the division. Some included the division commander, Maj. Gen. Throckmorton; Lt. Col. Emerson; Maj. Nelson Jones and his wife Mary Ellen; and 1st Lt. James Harris and his wife Doris, just to name a few.

In 1962 while I was assigned to Fort Bragg, missiles were identified just 90 miles off the coast of Key West, Florida. This caused interest at the highest levels. Before the situation was resolved, I was sent to Homestead Air Force Base in Florida as a coordinator and representative of the division. Maj. Jim Harris from the 82nd Airborne Division and I worked together on this operation, and it was there that I first met and worked with Col. Albert E. Milloy, who was assigned to the 82nd at the time.

The 82nd Airborne experience was a very challenging and interesting period in my military service career, but because most material I worked with was classified, it is one that I can't talk about.

On January 22, 1963, I was promoted to the temporary rank of Major. Then it was time to move on to the next assignment. This would take me to the Command and General Staff College (C&GSC) at Fort Leavenworth, Kansas where I was stationed from 1964 to 1965.

Peggy usually looked forward to new assignments, but it was always hard on both the boys to leave their friends. Nevertheless, they became good "army brats" and soon adapted.

C hapter 16
Command and General Staff College

The objective of the Command and General Staff College is to train officers for duty as commanders or staff officers. It represents all the armed services, and its students come from all branches of the military. It was a full year's course and required considerable study and commitment.

This assignment was a great time for the families of the students, and we made many lasting friendships. Air Force Major Fred Crow and his wife Mary, and Major Pete Costoff and his wife Midge were some of our closest friends. Major Joe Wilson and his wife Pat were also close, and Kent and Scott became very good friends with their children. Peggy and Midge studied oil painting and art together, and Peggy and I still have some of the pictures they painted then.

Besides the students who were being trained in the college courses of study, every member of each family was required to be prepared for the actions they needed to take when a cyclone alarm was sounded. Kansas is well known for this particular weather phenomenon. Although some touched ground nearby during that assignment, we never personally experienced one.

Promotion to Rank of Major

On September 27, 1965, my promotion and rank of Major became permanent.

Aloha!

Peggy and the boys were understandably quite excited and ready to go when I received orders for the next assignment — it was to the headquarters of the Commander-in-Chief Pacific (CINCPAC) at Camp Smith, a Marine base at Oahu, Hawaii.

C hapter 17
Hawaii (CINCPAC)

The assignment in Hawaii brought back many earlier memories of World War II, as Camp Smith (CINCPAC) is located just above Pearl Harbor on the island of Oahu.

There was one downside to the assignment. I was informed that there would be no base (military) housing available. This meant that I was on my own to arrange for housing for the family.

We mortgaged a small orange grove in Dover and raised the money to buy a house in Hawaii that had a swimming pool. It was on Iliwahi Loop in Kailua, the windward side of Oahu. A situation unique in Hawaii was that we could buy the house, but not the land – so, in actuality, we "owned" a mortgage.

Promotion to Lieutenant Colonel

Soon after arriving in Hawaii, we decided to enroll the boys in a private school named Punahou. The school had been established by missionaries, and it is an outstanding school that takes a student all the way from the first grade through the twelfth. According to our checkbook, it was expensive, but on November 4, 1966, I was promoted to Lieutenant Colonel, and that helped Peggy make ends meet and made it possible for the boys to attend the school.

We spent two enjoyable years in Kailua. Kent could swim, and it wasn't long before Scott could pick up just as many quarters off the bottom of the pool as Kent. Both boys, with Peggy's help and guidance, became excellent swimmers.

A Prologue to War

While all this was working out for Peggy and the boys, I was busy settling in to my new assignment, the Intelligence

Section of CINCPAC. Determining how to satisfy the Specific Intelligence Collection Requirements (SICRs) levied on CINCPAC by the Defense Intelligence Agency and by others tested my abilities to their fullest, and presented quite a challenge for me.

Gathering the information necessary to complete the SICRs took me all over the Pacific to places like Saigon in Vietnam, and to Thailand, Japan and Singapore, as well as to other destinations it is best not to mention. On these assignments, I had to leave Peggy, Kent and Scott behind for long periods.

In Vietnam, the enemy had not changed; it had both elements of the Viet Cong (VC) and the much larger and more formidable enemy combat units of the North Vietnamese Army (NVA).

When one is at war – and our country was definitely at war in Vietnam – one of the best sources of intelligence information comes from the debriefing of prisoners of war (POWs). Debriefing or interrogation of POWs will often reveal valid tactical and strategic information. The sooner the POW can be interrogated with the help of a translator, the more valid and useful the information obtained will be, particularly tactical information.

Because of the need to obtain information about the enemy's strength, plans and movements, the need to develop prisoner interrogation centers staffed with adequate translators became very clear. The South Vietnamese army interrogators became quite proficient.

This brief explanation provides, to some degree, my initial involvement in the war in Vietnam and its effect on Peggy and the boys while I was still stationed in Hawaii. When the war began to intensify, it became prudent to sell the house in Kailua and move to Fort Shafter where quarters were available. The Kailua house was sold and the move to Fort Shafter was accomplished.

Peggy's dad and mother visited us at Fort Shafter. From this high location, we could see Hickam Air Force Base in Hawaii, a really beautiful sight with the Pacific Ocean in the background.

Vietnam on the Horizon

It was predictable that the assignment at CINCPAC would terminate about a year after our move to Fort Shafter. The next tour of duty after CINCPAC would be to the combat zone in Vietnam for at least one year. When the year at Fort Shafter had gone by, the initial three-year assignment to Hawaii had been completed and I received orders for duty in Vietnam.

Separation

Peggy would have stayed in Hawaii, but her dad was not well. My orders provided for a delay en route to take the family back to Plant City. There, we bought a small house in the heart of town. Peggy quickly settled in and got the boys enrolled in Jackson Elementary School. Her mother and dad helped with the transition. The transition was also made a great deal easier by being in a town that was our birthplace, where it was easy to renew old friendships as well as make new ones.

Just to name a few old friends, these would include: Mac and Cookie Smith, Robert Parker, Jim and Dotty Pollock, Gene and Margaret Sikes, Ed and Myrtle Lou Swindle, David and Charlotte Walden, and Bruce and Patsy Carlton. We were thankful that Peggy would have so many friends on whom she could depend for support.

She also had several blood relatives from the Sparkman family living in the area.

The First United Methodist Church in Plant City where Peggy and I had been married played a big role in our lives.

Peggy's dad and a friend, Tina Coto, took the boys to the cabin in the Ocala National Forest for fishing and hunting. Their good friend David Walden took Kent and Scott to the father-son activities at the church and made sure they were involved in Little League. Gene Sikes helped the boys practice and compete for punt-pass-kick contests. Friends are a must when dad is overseas on assignment.

Goodbyes

Then once again, much too soon, we went through the parting rituals, each of us promising that *"These are not good-byes"* and *"I'll be gone for a year but I will return, you can depend on it!"*

At that time, the sincerity of the scout oath I took was tested, and my chance to demonstrate duty to God and my country and obedience to the scout law was at hand.

Chapter 18
Vietnam – Quan Loi

In September 1968 I arrived in Vietnam, where I was assigned to the First Infantry Division, the "Big Red One," also known as the "BRO." Elements of the 1st Division had arrived in Vietnam in July 1965, making it the first U.S. infantry force on the ground.

Upon arrival at Tan Son Nhut Air Base at Saigon, Vietnam, I found a note from Lt. Col. Joe Wilson. Joe and I had served together in Monterey, California; Jidda, Saudi Arabia; Command and General Staff College; Hawaii-CINCPAC; and now Vietnam. Joe was assigned to the 101st Airborne Division. Joe's note read:

> *"Ken, you should take off your shoes before you get in the bed where I slept last night. Al ham Dulilla!* ("Praise be to God" in Arabic). *Good Luck. Joe"*

A short period of processing at Di An and it was on to division headquarters at Lai Khe. There I met the division commander, Maj. Gen. Orwin C. Talbott, who had recently taken over as a replacement for Maj. Gen. Keith L. Ware, who had been killed in action just northwest of Quan Loi. Maj. Gen. Ware had been awarded the Medal of Honor for his service in Italy during World War II.

Assignment to the 1st Brigade

Gen. Talbott told me that I was being assigned to the 1st Brigade at Quan Loi, located on Highway 13, better known as Thunder Road. It is close to the Cambodian border area known as the "Fish Hook," a region about 75 miles northwest of Saigon.

I was taken by helicopter to Quan Loi, which is the operational base for the 1st Brigade. After taking off, I noted that the chopper gained altitude rapidly and stayed at about 2,000 feet for the entire trip, a flight path designed to avoid possible enemy ground fire. When we neared Quan Loi, the chopper descended quickly onto a pierced aluminum landing strip used by both helicopters and light, fixed-wing aircraft. The airstrip was surrounded by barbed wire revetments and several gun emplacements. The artillery appeared to be a mixture of 105, 155, and 8-inch firing positions.

Welcome to Quan Loi

As I left the helicopter, I heard a siren. While back at Lai Khe, I had been told a siren indicated that enemy rockets had been launched. The pilot of the chopper signaled me to take cover and then lifted off immediately. I found shelter and waited, hoping none of the incoming ordinance came my way. During the attack, which lasted for only about five minutes, I didn't observe anyone hit by rockets. I could hear explosions, but none hit right in my area.

Fire Base at Quan Loi 1969
a/k/a Rocket City

After a short time that seemed much longer than it actually was, the all clear signal sounded. I had now been formally introduced to Quan Loi.

After the all-clear, the brigade headquarters was pointed out to me as I grappled with my duffel bag, which contained my entire possessions for the one-year tour in country.

It wasn't long before I met a lieutenant colonel, the deputy brigade commander, who accompanied me to my living quarters. I dropped off the duffel bag, and the colonel gave me a quick briefing on our surroundings. He told me it was common for Gen. Talbott, the division commander, to assign more than one lieutenant colonel to the brigade. Lieutenant colonels were normally destined to be on the brigade commander's staff, but it was also possible one would be selected to become a battalion commander. In the Big Red One, officers were often evaluated for as long as six months before being designated as infantry battalion commanders.

That night, I met the current brigade commander, a full colonel who had just returned to headquarters. He had been away directing the insertion of two infantry battalions and a 105 artillery battery being deployed in his area of operations (AO). The three units were deployed near the Fish Hook area where NVA combat units spilled over into South Vietnam.

The NVA troops originated in Hanoi, the capital of North Vietnam, but to reach South Vietnam they traveled through Laos and then Cambodia to get to the Fish Hook area. Because the rules of enemy engagement prohibited attacking the NVA forces anywhere inside Cambodia, a sovereign nation, this meant that the NVA had a sanctuary throughout that entire country.

An Air Force forward air controller stationed at Quan Loi related to me one evening that when he flew night missions along the "friendly" side of the Cambodian border, he could see on the other side of the border at least 100 trucks with their headlights on, bringing NVA troops to the Fish Hook area.

Charlie Rogers

On another night at Quan Loi, Lt. Col. Charles C. Rogers of HHC-1-5 (HQ and HQ Co. of 1-5 Arty) engaged me in a long conversation about the employment of a 105 artillery battery (five guns (tubes)) in support of infantry units. I learned a lot from Charlie that night about his unit. Charlie had the reputation for being able to move the battery by chopper into an area and have them ready and firing in the shortest possible time.

The very next day after our conversation, Charlie was choppered out to his battery, which was assigned to support the infantry battalions. That night, one of the batteries was attacked by NVA forces who executed wave after wave of assaults on his position.

At one point, Charlie directed his battery to lower the guns and fire directly at the enemy with fletchettes, dart-shaped devices about three or four inches long.

fletchettes

The NVA attack inflicted numerous casualties, many being wounded severely enough to make them ineffective for further combat. Charlie himself was hit by enemy fire several times during the assault, but he steadfastly continued artillery support until shortly after dawn, when he passed out from loss of blood.

When the choppers came in to evacuate the wounded, it was clear that Charlie had performed over and above the call of duty. Charlie's actions that night kept the enemy from claiming victory in their attack and, indeed, the NVA forces suffered heavy losses. His hospitalization and extended recovery period were conducted back in the states.

Charlie was initially awarded the Distinguished Service Cross (DSC), the second highest award for valor. Charlie's DSC was later upgraded to the Medal of Honor, the highest award for valor, which is often personally awarded by the President of the United States at a ceremony in the oval office of the White House in Washington.

I feel it an honor to have known Charlie, a true hero.

Enemy Tactics

Occasionally, the day and night operations at the head-quarters would be interrupted by 122-rocket attacks. These rockets were point-detonating and would explode on contact with whatever they hit. Accordingly, you tried to get down "lower than a snake's belly" and prayed that the enemy didn't get a direct hit on you. You learned quickly not to run to a bunker seeking protection – those running would often become casualties – you just dropped where you were and hoped for the best.

Another tactic favored by the enemy was to steal as close as they could on foot, especially after nightfall, and try to breach the perimeter at Quan Loi. They were always repulsed, because the infantry defending Quan Loi established night defensive positions (NDPs) and were well dug in. The 105 artillery battery sandbagged their positions and were capable of direct or indirect fire against the enemy.

Brigade Duties

The brigade commander is in charge of the deployed infantry battalion and artillery units, and is directly responsible to the division commander. The brigade commander had many tasks for the extra lieutenant colonels assigned to Quan Loi, and one of the jobs that was assigned to me was monitoring radio transmissions from the deployed units, mostly at night. Other duties that might be assigned included the following:

1. Investigating casualties that were caused by choppers inserting patrols in prohibited areas. (If the choppers had had a global positioning system (GPS) available, this problem might have been eliminated.)

2. Daily inspections of perimeter defenses to prevent breaches by the enemy, a strategy they employed frequently.

3. Monitoring the tactical radio net.

4. Insuring the artillery batteries' preparedness for counteraction and their capability for responding to enemy rocket attacks in a timely manner.

5. Inspection of all types of activities that supported the brigade's mission.

6. Responding to any attack as directed by the brigade commander.

Terre Rouge

Collocated near the Quan Loi compound was a large house occupied by the French, who operated the Terre Rouge rubber plantation. (In English, "*Terre Rouge*" means "Red Earth.") Coordination with the Frenchmen to keep them reasonably informed of the Army's mission was an intriguing task.

Assignment to Rome Plow Operation

The Quan Loi base was taken over by an armored unit when the 1st Brigade moved to Lai Khe, although the mission of the 1st Brigade remained the same.

While serving at Lai Khe for a short period, I was tasked to represent the brigade commander as the coordinator for a new operation that was to eventually open the main road between Phuoc Vinh and Song Be. Engineer, infantry, artillery, Rome plows and support troops were heavily involved in this operation. I remained at Phuoc Vinh for an extended period before returning to Lai Khe.

Iron Rangers

On October 21, 1968, the armored personnel carriers (APCs, also called "tracks") of the 5/60 Infantry (Mech) were transferred to the Big Red One. Before the transfer, the 5/60th's AO was south of Saigon. After the transfer, their unit designation was changed to 1/16th Infantry (Mech), 1st Infantry Division, and they became known as the "Iron Rangers."

Change of Command

Lt. Col. Donald C. Shuffstall's battalion assumed command of the operation to open the road to Song Be, so I returned to Lai Khe. It was then that I learned the division commander, Maj. Gen. Talbott, would conduct a change of command ceremony at Lai Khe on April 8, 1969. I would be taking over from Col. Shuffstall.

The task force I would be responsible for in the days to come would include most of the units that I worked with at Phuoc Vinh. The new mission would be accomplished as a 1st Brigade unit, but in effect would be under the guidance of one of the assistant division commanders, Brig. Gen. Albert H. Smith.

Chapter 19
Vietnam – Rome Plow Operation

My first duty as commander of the 1st Infantry Battalion (Mech) was spent in the motor pool. Driving the armored personnel carriers under the guidance of motor pool mechanics was a new experience for me, as we were not taught about APCs at Fort Benning. The APCs were designed to transport an infantry squad, "buttoned up," to the final attack position under cover of artillery fire designed to kill enemy on the ground, then when the covering fire lifted, to exit the track and close with the enemy on foot to destroy or capture them. The APC's main armament is the .50-caliber machine gun.

In the BRO, the track was never buttoned up, as personnel preferred to fight from the top of the track. These mechanized infantry assumed the risks of such exposure to enemy fire in order to gain the advantages of better vision and early detection of the enemy. I would learn to appreciate this as I gained experience.

Rolling On

Two days after the change of command ceremony making me the new 1/16th commander, I would roll the Iron Rangers, riding on top of the tracks, to the field from Lai Khe.

The destination of the battalion was just east of Phuoc Vinh. The battalion was in the field to reopen Highways QL-14 and 311 to Song Be. This route traversed an area that had been under Viet Cong domination for the previous five to eight years, and II Field Force was anxious to reopen it.

The Viet Cong were South Vietnamese "turncoats" who assisted the North Vietnamese Army troops in inflicting casualties on the U.S. and South Vietnamese forces, and their units were constantly attacking supply convoys along the route.

The mission of my battalion was pure and simple: cut a 200-meter swath on each side of an old French highway for 40 miles between Phuoc Vinh and Song Be.

When the mission was accomplished, the Viet Cong's ability to conduct ambushes on supply convoys would be greatly diminished or perhaps even prevented. However, until the mission was accomplished in its entirety, the Viet Cong would be a constant threat. The job of the battalion's infantry was to protect the personnel in the task force until the mission was completed.

Widening the road necessitated the invention of a specialized tool for the job. American ingenuity came up with the Rome plow, a D-8 bulldozer with a flattened blade and a "stinger" used to fell trees too large to shear off next to the ground.

The Rome plow was engineered and constructed stateside in the city of Rome, Georgia, and technicians were sent in with the plows.

At one point in time during the land clearing operation, the engineers had 48 Rome plows in the cut at the same time. The norm was 24 to 36 in the cut.

example of a Rome plow with "stinger" blade

The engineers did a great job identifying and destroying mines that had been planted by the enemy in and around the roads. The appellation "Thunder Road" came about because of the noise the mines made when they exploded.

For the next three months, the battalion provided security for several U.S. and Army of the Republic of Vietnam (ARVN) engineer companies in some of the roughest terrain in the III CTZ.

About every eight days, the Iron Rangers constructed new fire support bases from which artillery and infantry could help protect the clearing operation. Additionally, in late May, Company "C" of the 1/16th (also called "Bandido Charlie"), commanded by Capt. Ken Costich, conducted search and destroy operations into the Phuoc Long Victory Gardens.

Capt. Costich invited me to accompany Bandido Charlie to the Victory Gardens, and I accepted. These ventures gave the battalion the distinction of being the first U.S. unit ever entering into these areas.

Modifying the APCs

General Smith was so proud of the 1/16 operation that he brought visitors out in his chopper to see them in action. Sometimes, he even brought visiting foreign dignitaries to see the Rome plows at work. Being overhead, he had a clear view of what was going on below. That scrutiny almost got me in trouble for approving a modification to the APCs to make them more efficient. There were several things that troubled me about the APC's but, primarily, it was the APC's weight.

1. The APC was too heavy, and it wasn't designed to bear the quantity of .50-cal. ammunition we were carrying. Since having even more ammunition on board was advantageous, reducing the amount of ammo was *not* an option.

2. Due to the weight, the torsion bars on the road wheels were being sheared off too rapidly, resulting in the loss of use of the APC during the time required for repairs.

3. Operating the locking lever on the .50-cal. turret was cumbersome. The locking lever had to be disengaged in order to rotate the turret, a very difficult thing to do when the APC was positioned on an incline and even more problematic and dangerous if the personnel on board were under enemy attack.

4. When enemy fire hit the steel protective plate behind the .50-cal. gunner, the bullets would ricochet off the plate and strike personnel on the track. If we removed the protective plate, that problem would be solved, and the weight of the APC would be greatly diminished as well.

On advice of my officers, and particularly on advice received from NCOs, a simple answer to the identified problem was found: remove the plate to reduce the weight. The NCOs supervised the removal of the plates on over 40 tracks that night and loaded the plates onto lowboys (flat-bed trailers) which were headed back to engineer headquarters near Saigon. The 40 tracks included those of Alfa and Charlie Companies.

The convoy of trailers traveling toward Saigon was observed by General Smith from his chopper. It wasn't long before he was landing and demanding to know "*Who* authorized the removal of so much steel from the APCs?" It was clear that the general was quite upset about what had been done.

Since I was in charge, it fell to me to answer his question. I replied quite simply, "I did, sir. And you authorized it when you told me I was responsible for all that my battalion does or fails to do."

After thinking for a minute or so about the reasons I gave him for the modification to the APCs, he said, "Your action makes sense. Good luck." He then went back to his helicopter and I went back to work.

The Open Road from Saigon to Song Be

My command operated in enemy territory 24 hours a day, seven days a week. The Viet Cong were very effective in their use of rocket propelled grenades (RPGs) and in choosing the time, place and circumstances for ambush. It should be noted that the RPG has the capability of penetrating 10 inches of homogenous armor, making it an effective and lethal weapon. A direct hit can shower molten metal inside an APC and anyone inside.

Looking back on the Rome plow operation — which was ultimately declared successful — let's examine it in detail to determine the various elements of the Task Force (TF) that contributed to this success.

The commander, 1st of the 16th Infantry Battalion, was responsible for the over-all conduction of the operation. The commander was to provide two artillery units, a 155 self-propelled artillery battery and a 105 artillery battery of 5 tubes. The concept was that as the Rome plows moved along the 40-mile route, these artillery units would be protected by either Alfa Infantry Company or by Charlie Company. As the TF moved along the established route, one of the artillery units would "leapfrog" over the other.

The artillery would conduct interdiction fire each night to keep the enemy Viet Cong off guard and possibly inflict casualties on them. Each infantry company would return to its fire base at night for protection of the base. Forward observers from artillery were provided by each infantry company. As a general rule, depending on the tactical situation, the artillery batteries would leapfrog every eight days.

Shortly after daylight each morning, the infantry companies would leave their fire base and take up positions to support the Rome plows. If the plows were not provided protection, the operation could fail, so the APCs (tracks) of each company would fall in line every fifth plow. Any track not assigned for this duty would stay in reserve for search and destroy missions, and this was also true for the few tanks assigned to the TF. The battalion deputy commander was responsible for assigning areas for search and destroy missions.

Maintenance of the Rome plows was the responsibility of the Rome plow company commander. The blades of the D-8 bulldozers had to be sharpened each night so that the plows would be ready for commitment the next morning. The honing of the blades created sparks which lit up the darkness each night — the enemy's favorite time for assault. In an effort to deter the VC from attacking the Rome plows and personnel while they were so highly visible and vulnerable, the infantry companies would periodically and randomly fire their .50-cal. MGs. This deterrent must have worked, because the Rome plows were never attacked at night.

So, when were we most vulnerable? It was when Alfa Company, Charlie Company, Headquarters elements, and the lowboys were transporting the Rome plows from point "A" to point "B," and the most vulnerable period was at dusk and at night when the VC had the advantage of cover of darkness.

A separate engineering effort was made to rebuild bridges and to clear mine fields, particularly along the designated route.

Helicopters were assigned to the TF for guiding the Rome plows as they widened the cut by 200 meters on each side of the main road. Once, when the helicopters were slow to refuel, one plow was unknowingly heading for Cambodia before it could be alerted to reverse its course. Communication was a must between the chopper and lead Rome plow.

Occasionally, a hot meal could be served, but not often. It was mostly "C" rations during the two and a half months of the operation. Complaints were never heard, as everyone in the task force knew that opening the road between Phuoc Vinh and Song Be was a mission that must succeed.

When I traveled by jeep from point "A" to point "B," the windshield was always lowered and the driver wore goggles to protect his eyes. Once, during the dry season, a cloud of dust appeared just to our front. Not knowing whether the dust was caused by the enemy, I pulled the trigger of my M-16 as I lowered the barrel. When we stopped, we discovered that the dust was caused by a 10-foot "aguana." An "aguana" looks similar to a Florida alligator. The "aguana" was killed, and the hood of the jeep received five hits just forward of the radiator. This is the first time I have ever admitted to  being responsible for the five holes in the front of the jeep! We picked up the "aguana" and gave it to the people at the next village we came to. "Aguana" is considered a delicacy to them, just as gator tail is considered a treat in Florida.

The task force completed the mission at Song Be, but even after being deemed a success there had been a price to pay for that success — in my opinion, a very heavy price. When it was completed, the Song Be road operation cost the battalion 10 killed in action (KIA), 67 wounded in action (WIA), and 10 APCs lost to enemy attacks.

On June 15, 1969, the first convoy from Saigon to Song Be ceremoniously rolled unmolested along the entire route, thus ending the domination of Phuoc Long Province by the VC

Song Be Bridge
This bridge represented the end of a mission - we reached the objective

Vietnam 1969
Lt. Col. Kenneth G. Cassels, 2nd from right
Capt. John J. MacNeill, Rome Plow Company C.O., 2nd from left
Brig. Gen. Albert H. Smith, Deputy C.G., 1st Inf. Div., 4th from left
brought five South American officers to visit Rome Plow operation
Gen. Smith later approved the assignment of Maj. James E. Harris
to 1st Battalion, 16th Inf., in July 1969

C hapter 20
Vietnam – Fire Support Base Jim

The 1/16 remained at Song Be for five days and then were sent to an area of operations near Lai Khe where Fire Support Base (FSB) Jim was established. An artillery battery and two mechanized infantry companies made up the elements stationed at FSB Jim.

Captain Phillip Greenwell was in command of "C" Company (a/k/a Charlie Company and "Bandido Charlie"), and Captain Robert Olson commanded Alfa Company. Both of these companies conducted Reconnaissance in Force (RIF) operations in this new AO.

It was during this period that the 1/16 welcomed Major James Harris as the Deputy Battalion Commander and Operations Officer of Headquarters Company (HQ). Jim and I had been together at the 18th Airborne Corps during the Cuban missile crisis in 1962.

Soon after his arrival, the battalion was turned over to him to command while I went on R&R to Hawaii. R&R was available to all personnel serving in Vietnam.

Peggy turned the boys, Kent and Scott, over to her mother and dad to look after and traveled from Plant City to Oahu. She met me there and we continued on to Kauai, the beautiful island where the movie *South Pacific* was filmed. Being together again was fantastic, but the five days ended all too quickly. Then it was back to Oahu. Peggy left Hawaii for Plant City and I headed back to Saigon.

Upon returning to FSB Jim, it took me most of the first night to tell Jim Harris about my R&R. I knew Jim's wife Doris would be interested, because Peggy and Doris were the best of friends.

An Loc

After a few short days at FSB Jim, on July 25, 1969, there was a surprise visit to our command post (CP) by the division commander, Major General Orwin C. Talbott. We knew that General Talbott had been selected to be the next commander of Fort Benning, Georgia, and he would be leaving Vietnam when his replacement arrived.

General Talbott told us that we had a 60-minute notice to get ready to move the battalion to the vicinity of An Loc, where Col. James Leach of the 11th Armored Cavalry Regiment (11th ACR) was waiting. We would receive further instructions from Col. Leach, who was to be our new commander, when we arrived there. General Talbott wished us well. In one hour we would be on the move.

Jim Harris and I formulated a quick plan. Jim would lead the battalion from Lai Khe along Thunder Road (Route 13) to An Loc. I would get overhead with my artillery fire support coordinator to provide cover for the 1/16 convoy. This movement began promptly at 1300 hours and would not be completed until 0500 hours the next day.

That day I spent 16 hours in the chopper. Fuel and relief chopper pilots were provided at Quan Loi. In the short periods when the helicopters were on the ground, Jim and his convoy would be without artillery support and vulnerable to attack. Fortunately, the enemy did not attack Jim's column.

The meeting with Col. Leach took place at 0500 hours as planned. His instructions were to continue moving our forces just past An Loc and to establish temporary NDPs. These positions would be held for several days.

Permanent positions were coordinated during the next couple of days, placing the 1/16, HQ and Charlie Companies at FSB Allons II, along with 155 and 105 artillery batteries and Alfa Company at FSB Eagle II, about eight kilometers north of An Loc. The 11th ACR was now stationed at Quan Loi.

President Nixon Visits the First Infantry Division

It was there where it was first learned that on July 30, 1969, the President of the United States, Richard M. Nixon, had flown to Vietnam and visited the BRO. This was a tremendous morale booster for our troops.

During President Nixon's 1969 round-the-world trip,
he took the time to talk with hundreds of enlisted men of
the First Infantry Division at Di An, Republic of Vietnam
July 30, 1969

Later, I received a letter and album from Gen. Talbott indicating that our 1/16 Bravo Company commander had been selected to protect the president. Captain Ernest Freeman, who was with us earlier on the Rome plow operation, was chosen.

The letter also informed me that LTC Vernon C. Coffey, Army Aide to the President and a former battalion commander with the BRO, accompanied President Nixon. Vernon and I had become good friends when he had led his battalion out of Quan Loi during the time I was there. The letter from General Talbott is included in its entirety at the end of this chapter.

Captain Ernest Freeman was the company commander of Bravo Company when the Rome plow operation began at Phuoc Vinh. He was with us until picked up by the division commander for another mission. Captain Robert Olson took command of Alfa Company when Ernest was transferred.

Tactical Intelligence on the 9th NVA Offensive

Instinctively, I knew that something big was about to happen. It was known that Thunder Road had been involved in several of the BRO actions against the 9th NVA Division. It wasn't long before my suspicions were realized.

In early August, it was learned that the 9th NVA Division commanded by Gen. Nguyen Thoi Bung was preparing for a new offensive in Binh Long Province. This unit was composed entirely of North Vietnamese regular armed forces straight from Hanoi. They would come via Laos and Cambodia and were planning to capture An Loc.

Intelligence indicators were that Bung's division might strike areas along Highway 13 between An Loc and Quan Loi from their base in Cambodia. That region was now the AO of the 3rd Brigade, 1st Cavalry Division, since that division assumed responsibility for Binh Long Province.

As I looked back and considered all the past training I had undergone and missions I had experienced to that point in time, I trusted that my scout training would carry me through the uncertainty that lay ahead. I said a prayer and hoped it would sustain me through whatever was to come.

HEADQUARTERS

FIRST INFANTRY DIVISION

OFFICE OF THE COMMANDING GENERAL
APO SAN FRANCISCO 96345

AVDB-CG   9 August 1969

Lieutenant Colonel Kenneth G. Cassels
Commanding Officer
1st Battalion, 16th Infantry
1st Infantry Division
APO San Francisco 96345

Dear Ken:

The 1st Infantry Division was deeply honored to be the only unit
visited on the Commander-in-Chief's visit to the Republic of Vietnam.
It was an event that will stand out in the Big Red One's long
history of firsts. The President's words, handshakes, and warm-
ing presence will also be long remembered by each of us individually.

President Nixon's compliments and encouragements were the very
best kind of morale boosters for the Division. All of us derived
a sense of pride and accomplishment from the President's now-
famous words: "I think history will record that this may have been
one of America's finest hours, because we took a difficult task
and we succeeded."

You are to be commended for the part your outfit played in the
drama of 30 July. Let me extend to you and your men a sincere thank
you for representing the Division so well.

To preserve some of the highlights of President Nixon's visit to the
1st Infantry Division we have put together this album. Please accept
it with my deep appreciation.

Sincerely,

ORWIN C. TALBOTT
Major General, USA

Chapter 21
Vietnam – Operation Kentucky Cougar

When the shift in the area of operations occurred, Colonel James Leach, 11th Armored Cavalry Regiment, was placed under the control of the 1st Cavalry Division. To thwart the 9th NVA Division's plans to capture An Loc, Major General Elvy B. Roberts, Commander of the 1st Cavalry Division, initiated *Operation Kentucky Cougar*.

For this operation, the 1st Battalion, 1st Infantry Division, was placed under the operational control of the 11th ACR. Effectively, this put the 1/16 "on loan" from the BRO to the 1st Cavalry Division.

This was the reason for establishing the 1/16 at FSB Allons II on Highway 13; it was there to help Gen. Roberts block the eastward movement of the 272nd and 273rd regiments of the 9th NVA Division.

The Battle of Binh Long Province

The battle of Binh Long Province really began when the 1/16 moved to the vicinity of An Loc from FSB Jim. During the next 30 to 60 days, the Iron Rangers would fight two major actions and numerous smaller engagements.

The first action was in response to an incursion by elements of the 272nd NVA Regiment near An Loc. Initially, it appeared that this unit was headed toward either Quan Loi or An Loc.

10 August 1969

On 10 August 1969, a platoon from Captain Phillip Greenwell's Bandido Charlie Company conducted an air assault near An Loc. This operation, under the leadership of

Lt. George Perabo, was in coordination with an ARVN company from the 4th Battalion, 9th ARVN Regiment. The combined U.S./ARVN force pushed forward and into a landing zone (LZ) defended by the NVA troops. Upon landing, the Bandidos immediately engaged the NVA unit and killed 23. Four enemy soldiers were captured in hand-to-hand combat.

Overhead in the command helicopter, I saw the entire action unfold below. Considering that the Bandidos had done more than their share of the fighting, I told the ARVN commander riding with me in the chopper that "We're going in, and you will take over the fight. I'm pulling the Bandidos out of there." The chopper pilot was instructed to put us down, and he got close enough so that my radio operator and I could jump off. The ARVN commander got off at the same time.

That was the *hottest* LZ that I was ever in, and I'm sure the chopper took bullets as it rose from the LZ.

Upon landing, I found that there were four prisoners of war with their hands tied behind their backs being guarded by the Bandidos. Later that same day, the POWs were interrogated and revealed that they indeed were elements of the 272nd NVA Regiment.

The interrogation further yielded the information that the 273rd was also at the Cambodian border and poised to come into South Vietnam. Their combined mission was to capture the provincial capital of An Loc.

The POWs didn't know the exact number of NVA forces, but kept saying it was a very, *very* large force. This information was the best human intelligence any military commander could ask for.

After dark that same evening, Maj. Gen. Roberts, commander of the 1st Cavalry Division, landed his chopper on Highway 13 across from FSB Allons II, and I went across the berm to meet him. This was the first and only time I ever saw Gen. Roberts.

He congratulated me on a fine air assault mission and expressed his thanks for the new intelligence gathered from the prisoners captured that day. He also informed me he was awarding me the Silver Star medal. I responded that I didn't deserve it – that the Bandidos were the only ones deserving the honor. Perhaps he later thought over what I said and agreed with me, because I never received that Silver Star.

On the afternoon of 11 August, I briefed my battalion on the impending operation. All were placed on the highest alert. Because of the diminished size of the Iron Rangers for the upcoming operation, Col. Leach gave me D Company from the 5th Battalion, 7th Cavalry, to provide supplemental firepower. Even with the additional rifle company, I would be leading just over 300 men.

That same afternoon, I was directed by Col. Leach to take my force to the vicinity of FSB Eagle II and from there to attack the NVA enemy forces that had been identified by the prisoners captured on 10 August.

12 August 1969

Moving in the darkness, the battalion elements linked up at Eagle II some two hours before dawn on 12 August. The enemy had withdrawn sometime before we arrived, so I decided to move along their suspected withdrawal route.

As I planned the coming maneuver, I recalled when I had taught military history and the principals of war at the University of Connecticut at Waterbury. It had occurred to me back then that George Washington crossed the Delaware River and proceeded to engage the Hessians, a German mercenary force allied with England, at daybreak. The enemy force was drunk after partying all night on Christmas day. Since they were drunk, it was easier for Washington the next morning to kill several, and he captured some 300. This action changed the outcome of the Revolutionary War.

This vision of gaining such a tactical advantage was why I moved my force at night and insisted that the contact with the NVA enemy should occur at daylight. In all my training and experience, I had never heard of three rifle companies being committed at dawn before, but I believed the advantages to be gained by doing so were great and I determined to accomplish it.

Two mechanized infantry companies and one "leg" company ("grunts") were committed at dawn. And, too, never before had I heard of forty .50-cal. machine guns with supporting weapons being committed against a known enemy. Perhaps it may be a record for a mechanized infantry battalion with "grunts" to support this type of commitment. If we were successful in making the enemy contact occur at dawn, it would give us all day to fight the battle that lay ahead.

The Iron Rangers moved out, with Olson's Alfa Company leading, Greenwell's Charlie Company following, and troops of the 7th Cavalry riding on the tops of the Bandidos' APCs.

Encountering a suspicious stream crossing, Olson's lead platoon took an inordinate amount of time to reconnoiter the area before going across. At a standstill and becoming impatient with the delay, I went forward to get the column moving again. The meeting at the ford was friendly, but the lieutenant got the message I conveyed during our conversation, and moved on across the three-inch-deep stream.

I joined the column about four APCs back from Alfa Company's lead platoon. The rest of Alfa Company followed, then the Bandidos with the 7th Cavalry unit.

At about 0705 hours, after traveling approximately four kilometers, the lead platoon of Alfa Company was hit by RPGs and automatic weapons fire. The platoon leader's track took the first RPG and just seconds later was struck again by a 57-mm recoilless round that killed the driver and set the APC on fire, which I could see billowing with black smoke. The platoon leader was blown clear of the track, dazed but not injured. Also thrown clear were the .50-cal. gunner and the other personnel on the track.

As soon as the lieutenant recovered somewhat, he made his way back to my track to report the situation and to let me know that his driver had been killed. Assuring him that I had seen the attack on his track, I expressed regret that his driver had been killed. I told him that we had, in all probability, stumbled upon the main body of the 272nd Regiment of the 9th NVA Division. I directed him to mount another of his platoon's APCs and get a base of fire started against the enemy, forcefully pointing out that if he didn't, we would *all* be killed. He was a good officer and reacted immediately.

Though I made every effort not to show it, I too was afraid and my stomach was doing backflips. In my mind, I hearkened back to the captured POWs' assertions that the 272nd was a big, *big* NVA force. I knew then that I had led the bravest soldiers in the world into hell – that hell being approximately 600 or more regular NVA forces straight out of Cambodia – all fresh, highly trained and well armed troops.

Even considering the most conservative number of NVA forces, we were outnumbered at least two to one. Despite "shaking in my boots," I deployed the rest of Alfa Company, all the Bandidos and the 7th Cavalry unit to attack; Alfa company on the left, Charlie Company on their right, and the cavalry unit protecting our rear and flanks. I would take a position between Alfa and Charlie during the attack.

The enemy was dug in, and they were up in the rubber trees firing directly at the men on the APCs. The enemy's employment of rocket-propelled grenades was steadily increasing. Our .50-cal. machine guns laid down a base of fire and the mechanized infantry added their personal arms fire to that of the guns. The mechanized forces fought mostly from the APCs. The "grunts" always left the tracks as soon as possible and fought from the ground. Their M-16 weapons were very effective against the enemy in the trees as well as those on the ground.

Off and on during the battle, there well may have been as many as forty or more .50-cal. guns firing at the same time. Fortunately, for the most part, the enemy did not have .50-cal. machine guns.

Enemy fire continued to increase, and the advance of the 40 APCs of the battalion slowed or stopped completely. Even though I radioed many times for artillery support, it never came. Radio transmissions didn't always get through, and in any event the thick overhead canopy of the trees in the rubber plantation where the battle was taking place may have made the use of tactical air support questionable. The reason may never be known.

After about 40 minutes of intense fighting, my driver was hit by AK-47 machine gun fire, inflicting a compound fracture of his right arm, and he was bleeding profusely. Despite being badly wounded, he tried to drive the APC with one hand, which is almost impossible. As he pulled on one lever and raced the engine, the response was similar to a slingshot: it catapulted me off the track.

The APC went on, leaving me flat on the ground trying to avoid enemy fire while attempting to recover my operations maps. By that time, other personnel on my track were able to stop it and had called in a medic, who was administering first aid to my driver and arranging to take him to the rear (wherever the "rear" was) for evacuation out by chopper. My driver was an outstanding soldier, and he and I had become very close.

I managed to avoid getting hit by enemy fire while on the ground. I recovered my maps and finally got back on my track. At this point, I knew that the Alfa Company commander had been hit, but the extent of his injuries was not known. Everyone still on the Bandido Charlie track had been seriously wounded except for Captain Phil Greenwell himself, who was even then trying to encourage his men to *fight like hell*.

All personnel in this 300-soldier task force of the 1/16 showed courage, resolve, and determination to win the fight.

The NVA force was very good, but our men were better and fiercely determined. Though I was already aware of many things from personal observation during past operations, I was now absolutely certain of what can't be judged with the eyes – these well-trained soldiers were resourceful, courageous men who were "gutsy" beyond belief, even under extreme combat conditions. I was so proud of them all.

Fierce fighting continued, with give-and-take maneuvering on both sides. It seemed that the enemy must have had a *zillion* RPGs at their disposal. By mid-afternoon, my track had been disabled by enemy RPG fire. The same was true of the Alfa and Charlie commanders' tracks. All three of us scrambled to other tracks to continue the fight. Soon the enemy force attempted to flank the battalion, but the Iron Rangers countered the move and contained the attempt.

By noon, three more APCs had been knocked out of action, but the battle waged on.

At about 1400 hours, one of the battalion's command and control choppers carrying the battalion's deputy commander, Major James Harris, was shot down. Jim was uninjured and was rescued, and by 1500 hours was back in the air attempting to help in the battle.

Fighting continued until 1600 hours, when Col. Leach directed the battalion to break contact and go back to protect the artillery units on the fire bases.

Aftermath

Our battle on 12 August 1969 against the NVA forces lasted nine hours and was fought by the most heroic and gutsy soldiers in the world. I pray that my leadership on that day measured up to those actions taken by so many unidentified brave and courageous leaders on the battlefield.

The next day, 13 August 1969, the battalion went back to the area where the battle had been conducted. There we observed many blood trails, body parts stuffed in holes, and drag marks where a lot of bodies had been dragged away. This was often done by the NVA after a battle, and they followed that procedure here because they didn't want it known how successful the 1/16 and supporting units had been.

Although no one will ever know for certain exactly how many of the enemy were killed, the fighting cost the Iron Rangers two killed in action, 27 wounded in action and 6 APCs destroyed.

Another indicator of the battalion's win in spite of the overwhelming odds was three separate incidents observed when three enemy soldiers, believed to be NVA officers, exposed themselves to our tracks, pulled the pin on a grenade and deliberately blew themselves up. I say it was deliberate, because not one even attempted to toss his grenade toward the tracks. Perhaps they had "lost face" and this was their way out of disgrace. No one will ever know.

It was on this day that I learned of a selfless action by Brigadier General Herbert E. Wolff, the assistant division commander of the Big Red One. He heard on the morning of 12 August that there were several wounded. Though not in the BRO's area of operations, he came and helped evacuate the injured soldiers. He is owed a debt of appreciation for his aid.

With humility and deep gratitude, I thank all of those who participated or were involved in the 12 August 1969 battle.

5 September 1969

The other significant battle involving the Iron Rangers took place on 5 September 1969 as part of *Operation Kentucky Cougar*. Once again, Alfa Company and Bandido Charlie Company were engaged in a firefight, this time with a large portion of the other NVA regiment, the 273rd. Here is how it happened.

At about 1330 hours, our battalion's S-2 (intelligence officer) and elements of the 1st Platoon, Alfa Company, were dispatched to the compound of the 214th Regional Forces Company to conduct interviews with its members regarding an enemy attack on their compound the night before. Upon completion of the interviews, the Iron Rangers were en route back to the battalion NDP at Allons II when they were ambushed.

Jim Harris and I were at our command post when the transmission came in to *Devour 6* (my radio call sign):

Devour 6, this is Devour 2. I can now tell you where the enemy is, over.

Devour 2, this is Devour 6. Where is the enemy, over.

This is 2 – all around me – help!

Devour 2 – we're on our way! Out.

I responded by mounting Alfa and Charlie Companies and racing for the ambush site. Once there, we spotted the beleaguered 1st Platoon, and I immediately deployed the companies: Greenwell's Bandidos were on the right and Alfa Company was on the left. As some 25 or more APCs went into action, the troops could see the gun flashes of many AK-47s engaging them on their left front.

Once the link-up was achieved, I swung the two companies to the southwest and began engaging the enemy. Greenwell's company received the majority of the rifle fire, and he gradually moved his unit forward to hose down the NVA positions with .50-cal. machine gun fire.

Alfa Company refused its left flank after receiving RPG fire across the road to its left. Moreover, the company had not kept up with the forward movement of the Bandidos. Before long, some of Alfa Company's fire began to hit in and near the tracks of the Bandidos. Realizing the imminent danger of fratricide, I yelled over the battalion command radio for Alfa Company to pull forward. They failed to respond, and perhaps there were transmission problems. It couldn't be determined whether anyone heard these commands, but judging by their lack of response it appeared that they had not. The danger created by this situation became critical in a very short time.

This is where the courageous actions of the battalion operations noncommissioned officer, Master Sergeant Stephen Rabourn, came into play. He also recognized the gravity and danger of the situation and realized that my radio must have been nonoperational. He said, "Sir, I'll take care of it." He then jumped off the command track and raced to resolve the problem with both companies. During his daring action, he was hit three times by enemy fire.

While the sergeant was off the track, my .50-cal. gunner and three soldiers riding with us were busy doing their share of the fighting. One of them spotted an enemy RPG team about to launch a missile at our track and hollered at me to duck. Before they could put the two NVA soldiers out of commission, the enemy fired the missile and the RPG sped on its way toward us. We were extremely fortunate that it missed our track, going right over my head and finally hitting a tree to my left. When the RPG exploded on the tree, I was hit with shrapnel from the explosion.

The soldiers on my track then assured me, "Don't worry, sir, we killed both of them."

I was bleeding but not out of the fight, which continued until about 1830 hours.

Back to Base

It was dark when we returned to Allons II. There the 1/16 Battalion medical doctor carefully extracted the shrapnel from my left elbow, put on a very impressive bandage, and gave me a tetanus shot.

We were fortunate to have a medical doctor assigned to the fire support base at Allons II. The men injured in the fight who required further medical treatment were evacuated to hospitals; the rest were treated, as I was, by the battalion medical doctor at Allons II.

In this engagement, the battalion suffered two soldiers killed, 54 wounded, and a couple of APCs destroyed.

An investigation of the incident directed by Col. Leach, 11th ACR, later revealed that no American troops were injured by "friendly fire." The actions taken by Master Sergeant Rabourn to avert the pending crisis had been completely successful. He was awarded the Silver Star for his heroism, then evacuated to a hospital for treatment of his numerous wounds.

Just as on 12 August 1969, it was impossible to determine how many enemy forces were destroyed. It is safe to say that heavy enemy casualties were inflicted, and the effectiveness of the 9th NVA Division had been greatly reduced.

Success at a Price

By the end of *Operation Kentucky Cougar*, some estimates credit the 1/16 Battalion with killing 150 NVA troops in some of the heaviest fighting of the year.

These engagements were a major setback to the 9th NVA Division plans and prevented its anticipated attacks on An Loc and Quan Loi, but they also cost our battalion 4 KIAs, 62 wounded, and 8 APCs.

A good part of my ability to lead forces in combat can be traced back to becoming an Eagle Scout in Plant City, Florida. I believed then, as I do now, that the scout oath, if followed, will lead one to acceptable actions in combat.

C hapter 22
The Big Red One

As my one-year tour with the Big Red One was about to terminate, I reflected on what Gen. Talbott had said to me just six months before. The words he used had been received with deep humility and honor. He said: "Ken, go lead the First Battalion, 16th Infantry."

The battalion consisted of officers, non-commissioned officers (NCOs), and draftees. The draftees made up at least 90% of the combat force. The U.S. government directed, with some exceptions, that physically qualified 18-year-olds would serve in the armed forces for two years. For lack of a better term, this was generally referred to as a draft.

Draftees assigned to the infantry would undergo training the first 12 months. The second 12 months they would be committed to combat. During this period of combat, for the most part, these brave and committed soldiers were, on average, 19 years of age. When the draftees completed their two-year commitment, they would be returned home to civilian life.

The officers, NCOs and draftees all served the United States with honor and distinction. Their service to the United States of America was marked with blood and sacrifice —

"They all gave some – some gave all."

There was a reminder to all of us in country of the price some might have to pay; it was printed on the sign in front of division headquarters at Lai Khe, Vietnam. It read:

"Danger Forward"

It was an honor for me to lead such honorable, dedicated and courageous men of the 1st Battalion, 16th Infantry, 1st

Infantry Division. Eleven soldiers in the 1st Division were awarded the Medal of Honor for their service above and beyond the call of duty in Vietnam.

Soon after September 1969, the 1st Cavalry Division terminated *Operation Kentucky Cougar*, and that day the Iron Rangers rolled south on Highway 13 in a cold, soaking rain.

As the Iron Rangers approached the north gate of Lai Khe after a long, wearisome road march led by Major Jim Harris, troops on the lead tracks heard band music. Then they spotted the new division commander, Major General Albert E. Milloy, all the division staff, and the Big Red One band standing at the gate. General Milloy and his staff were there to welcome the brave and courageous Iron Rangers home. I wasn't in a position to witness this historic event, as I was overhead in my role as artillery support for Jim Harris if he needed it on the trek home.

After their arrival, the troops found barbecued chicken, steaks, potato salad, and plenty of other good food waiting for them.

It was good to see Gen. Milloy again, as we had served together when he was a full colonel with the 82nd Airborne Division during the Cuban missile crisis in 1962. That night he invited me over to division headquarters for dinner and thanked me for a job well done.

Two days later Gen. Milloy conducted a change of command ceremony, with Lt. Col. David C. Martin assuming command of the 1st Battalion, 16th Infantry (Mechanized) from me. The ceremony was witnessed by Col. Leach and by the Iron Rangers standing proudly in formation. I was presented the Legion of Merit. David Martin would be in command for only a few days before the Iron Rangers rolled to the field again.

The day after the change of command ceremony, I was summoned to division headquarters where Gen. Milloy showered me with Vietnamese awards and decorations. He also presented a couple of Silver Stars, a Bronze Star, 11 Air Medals, and a firm handshake. He wished me well in my new assignment to the Pentagon. A division chopper stood by, waiting to take me to Saigon for the welcome flight home.

Thus ended my tour with the Big Red One —

No mission too difficult
No sacrifice too great
Duty first

C hapter 23
The Pentagon

Upon entering the "golden bird" at Tan Son Nhut in Saigon, my emotions were mixed. During the first few hours, my thoughts mostly went back to those daring and courageous 19-year-olds and others who made it possible for me to be on this "golden bird" making the trip home. That is a bond that can never be broken. Those men, mostly draftees, served their country in an outstanding manner. When their commitment of two years was finished, most of them would return to being civilians. Some would go on to higher education; some would take up new skills and be civilians that America could be proud of. Wherever their paths may take them and however they are treated upon returning to America, I wish them well!

Reunited

Where the "golden bird" touched down in America is not important. My thoughts were focused solely on Peggy, Kent and Scott. At the end of the long journey, there I was – home at last in Plant City, and there were Peggy, Kent and Scott.

This homecoming was warm and wonderful, and I felt at peace for the first time in a long while. Soon we were joined by Peggy's mother and dad. We all cried, but it was with emotions of joy and with no shame or apologies for the tears.

Peggy, with her usual efficiency, had already made all the arrangements for our next challenge: duty at the Pentagon. While her mother and dad kept Kent in Little League baseball, she took Scott and boarded a train to Washington, D.C. where Brig. Gen. Robert (Bob) Koch and his family met them at the train station. Gen. Koch had been our neighbor in Hawaii when we were both stationed at CINCPAC.

Gen. Koch helped Peggy find a house that we could afford through a VA loan, which was the only way we could afford to buy a house anywhere. It was a three-bedroom house that bordered the Army/Navy country club in Fairfax City, Virginia. Peggy had also made all the arrangements for selling the house in Plant City. How proud I was of her and everything she had accomplished – now we could relax and *enjoy* the 30-day delay en route to the new assignment!

Eventually, the moving truck arrived to take our furniture to the new house. Goodbyes are never easy, but this time as I left friends behind it was to say, with more certainty, "*I'll see you later.*" My dearest ones – my family – and I would make this trip together.

Scott and Peggy had already seen the new house. When we saw it, Kent and I were overjoyed with their selection of such a beautiful house to call home. Getting settled in the new house was fun, and it was also time to get the boys in school and to meet new friends.

Some new friends included Clay and Betty Ann Ritter and their daughters. Betty Ann and Peggy had grown up together in Plant City. They were only a few blocks away. Clay had been employed in Plant City with the local Agriculture Department and was now part of the national agricultural organization. Charles and Pat Anderson and their beautiful twin daughters lived only two doors away. He was an Air Force officer stationed in the Pentagon. Lee and Jo Minnis lived across the street.

When leave was over, it was time to put the uniform back on and travel to the Pentagon. It was time to go back to work.

Surprise Reception

As I parked in the Pentagon's parking lot, I could see a large crowd that had gathered at the entrance to the building. As I approached the entrance, I passed through a cordon of federal marshals who were trying to control the crowd, a mob that was shouting obscenities and throwing cow dung at me. It was evident they were not pleased with the war in Vietnam.

The mob was venting their anger on a closer target — the soldiers who were returning home from fighting the war. No one in the crowd apparently stopped to think, or perhaps didn't even care, that the soldiers they attacked so viciously had simply been serving their country.

I was told that an infantry company had already been stationed in the Pentagon in case it became necessary to use force to protect the Pentagon and its personnel.

I learned that Washington was *on fire* in several areas.

This was not at all the *"home*coming" I might have expected from America. In Vietnam, we lived in enemy territory all the time and did not have television to keep us informed of what was going on back in the states. After facing an enemy on foreign soil, we now faced enmity at home.

I couldn't help but think about the brave men I had left behind in Vietnam, and what a shame it was that they might have to face the same kind of greeting on their arrival home. I reminded myself often and kept thinking, *"No mission too difficult – no sacrifice too great – duty first."*

On the Job

So I went on with my duty, beginning my assignment with the Security Division of the Assistant Chief of Staff for Intelligence.

Traversing the building from point "A" to point "B" was accomplished through five separate rings with hallways in between each ring. A total of 17 miles of corridor wound through the Pentagon.

A full colonel (06) would be my direct supervisor. My portion of the intelligence "pie" was manned with mostly civilians who were experts in their field. They all had general service (GS) ratings that ranged between GS 10 and GS 13. Secretaries were assigned and stationed at various locations so they could cover any sections as needed. Secure filing cabinets were located in each office to protect the classified material contained therein.

The civilians were literary experts in their field of handling information which had to be protected in the interest of national security. These were the folks who directed the investigations of Army personnel who, it was believed, would have a "need to know" classified information in connection with their service assignments. They made the final decisions as to whether or not that person was cleared to read and handle classified material.

Now I understood why I had been required to pull KP for so long at Scott Field in Illinois during WWII – it was so that an investigation could be conducted into my background. My clearance for exposure to top secret information had been a requirement for attendance at cryptography school.

While at the Pentagon, I completed professional courses connected with my assignment there, including the National Communications Security course and the Industrial Security Orientation course.

It took me a while to determine where I fit into the scheme of things in Intelligence Security. It finally occurred to me that some Army regulations pertaining to classified material, specifically Army Regulation 380-5, required the classification of a great deal of information that did not need any such protection. Perhaps that is why in July 1966, President Lyndon Johnson signed into law the Freedom of Information Act passed by Congress.

We knew the national archives contained row after row of classified material. Some of the information was designated for protection for valid reasons, and those reasons would continue beyond the current era. Certainly, the methods of acquiring the information and the sensitive sources of that information had to continue being protected for an extended period of time. If not protected, the individuals providing the information and the methods of acquiring it could cost some of them their lives.

It was known that a large percentage of classified material contained in the national archives could be declassified, provided that sensitive sources and methods could be identified for exemption from declassification. Human intelligence in particular must be identified and protected. There were units in the Army Reserves whose members were intelligence specialists, and several of these units were activated to work with the national archives to declassify Army information that no longer needed protection. The specialists also identified the materials that must remain protected. This kept many reservists in the intelligence field busy for many months.

This process seemed like a good concept. However, there is much in the archives that is not limited to Army matters. What about information that needed to be protected for the Navy, Marines, Coast Guard, Air Force, or government agencies?

Implementation of the declassification program required a higher authority than just that of the Army; it required the Department of Defense to take action and direct all regulations to be written that would pertain to all divisions of service, not just the Army. Accordingly, a large part of my day was spent working with intelligence personnel of other branches of service, all overseen and directed by Department of Defense personnel.

When my section of the new Army Regulation 380-5 was rewritten and implemented, I was directed to take the new regulation to the field, in Europe and elsewhere. I would explain it and suggest implementation by the appropriate commands.

Master Sgt. Stephen Rabourn

It was on this trip that a master sergeant named Stephen Rabourn, then stationed in Germany, approached me and asked if I remembered him. He had a big smile on his face. My reply was:

Of course! How could I forget the operations master sergeant who worked with Major James Harris? On 5 September 1969, you joined my track and we were involved in the attack against the 273rd NVA Regiment, relieving the pressure on Alfa Company personnel.

You're the one who jumped off the track when my communications equipment failed and said, "Sir, I'll take care of it," and you did. You prevented the possibility of friendly fire from taking place. You were hit three times that day by enemy fire, and refused treatment 'til we put you on a chopper going to the hospital. You were also given the Silver Star for your actions on that day.

By the way, Sergeant, have you ever run into that tall, blue-eyed blonde that we saw with the NVA forces on 5 September 1969?

Sgt. Rabourn replied:

Yes, Sir, he is here in Germany and he is with the Russian embassy. We had dinner together in Berlin. He confirmed that he was one of the Russian advisers to the 9th NVA Division on 5 September 1969.

Our conversation continued, and I recalled:

After you left my track that day, elements of the 273rd NVA Regiment fired an RPG at my APC—it passed over my head and hit a tree on my left. I received shrapnel in the elbow from the RPG that hit the tree. The men on my right killed the two NVA soldiers who fired it.

When we parted, I told him, "Sergeant, it was so good to see you again." And it was.

While in Germany conducting briefings on the new regulations, I met with Brigadier General David C. Martin, who had taken my place in Vietnam. He had moved up in rank rapidly and now commanded a unit in Stuttgart, Germany. After meeting with Gen. Martin, my mission was completed and I returned to the Pentagon.

Pinning the Eagles

My tour in the Pentagon was not all work. Most weekends were free, and once in a while it was possible to go home to Fairfax City and watch the boys play in Little League. Both boys were heavily involved in the Boy Scouts, so I sometimes went with them on camping trips, really enjoyable occasions for all of us. Part of the weekend included going to church on Sunday and enjoying a nice meal together as a family.

The most significant thing that happened during the Pentagon assignment occurred on 12 July 1972 when I was promoted to full Colonel. Peggy brought both of the boys to watch the ceremony, which was conducted by a brigadier general and the Assistant Chief of Staff for Intelligence. Kent and Scott had big grins on their happy faces as they watched Peggy pin the "Eagle" on one of my shoulders. The general pinned the other side. This promotion was made possible because of the courageous and brave men of the 1st Battalion, 16th Infantry (Mech), the Iron Rangers.

Peggy planned a big party at our home in Fairfax City to celebrate my promotion. The guest list included a Bandido Charlie, Phil Greenwell; Lt. Col. James Harris and his wife Doris; and our neighbors, Lee and Jo Minnis and Pat and Charles Anderson. My mother was also able to come from Florida to attend the party. Kent and Scott enjoyed this festivity even more than the pinning of the eagles.

The Pentagon tour was rewarding, as it taught me to be thankful that our country is strong and that for it to remain strong it must have superb leadership. At the Pentagon, I met many who would qualify. I was proud to be a part of it, proud to be raised in Plant City, Florida, and proud to be a part of the leadership for this country.

While in Fairfax, in June 1973 I was cited for steadfast service to Boy Scout Troop 882, a citation of which — may I say it? — I am quite proud.

C hapter 24
Atlanta, Georgia

New orders took us from the Pentagon to Atlanta, Georgia. Even then, Atlanta had the largest airport in the Southeast and was a major hub for flights heading out in many directions all over the United States and elsewhere.

The Army was undergoing major command structure changes to meet new challenges resulting from the abolishment of the draft. Training of the all-volunteer Army included influencing the Army National Guard and the Army Reserve forces to become combat ready. My new unit was located at the Atlanta Army Depot and was designated as Headquarters-Army Readiness Region IV (ARR IV). Our boss was Major General Matheson, a WWII combat veteran. The headquarters included specialists from most branches of the Army.

Infantry Coordinator

My job was Infantry Coordinator for the Army National Guard and Special Forces units in Alabama, Georgia, Florida, Tennessee, Mississippi and Puerto Rico. The National Guard trained once a month on weekends and two weeks during the summer months.

It didn't take long to convince the units that combat preparedness was the name of the game. It also didn't take long for me to learn that there were a lot of outstanding leaders among the ranks of the "weekend warriors." The leaders, by and large, had little or no combat experience, but all were dedicated and anxious to talk to those who had experienced combat. Many had volunteered for schooling at Fort Benning or, in the case of the senior officers, Command and General Staff College. The Special Forces units' morale was high, as it is in most jump units. (The increase in jump pay *may* have accounted for some of this morale boosting!)

A Great House

That explains the mission to be accomplished, but what about the family? As usual, Peggy was ahead of me – she had contacted real estate agents in Atlanta prior to leaving Washington. She had several options in mind for a house and had looked into the school situation as well. She made a quick decision on both housing and school, based on the expectation that my Atlanta assignment would last for at least two years. Kent would graduate from high school during the time we would be in Atlanta. The assignment might last even longer, as there was a very large Army headquarters at Fort McPherson in Atlanta for future assignment possibilities. In that case, Scott might also finish school while we were there.

Planning ahead, Peggy looked into the potential options and settled on a three-bedroom house in the DeKalb County area of Atlanta. It was a two-story brick house, perhaps the best house we had ever lived in. It was just a short distance to my assigned duty station and close to the best school in the area.

The house in Georgia was ideal. The distance to work had not changed, but the name of our headquarters was changed to Fort Gillem. The house had a large basement that we converted into a bedroom for Kent. He appreciated the additional bath and the privacy. A pool table was in the basement, next to a fireplace heated by propane gas. Both boys enjoyed that area!

Peggy was happy there, even though I would be on the road the better part of the year and gone almost every weekend. Kent and Scott were very much involved in the Georgia soccer program. Fortunately, since their games were played during the week, I was able to attend some of them.

Catching a Curve Ball

In the spring of the year, this all changed unexpectedly when Gen. Matheson walked into my office and said, "Ken, I have a problem in Florida, and since you are from Florida I was wondering if you would consider going down there and straightening it out."

As the Infantry Coordinator for the State of Florida, I was already aware that the three infantry battalions in the Florida National Guard were not entirely on board with the Readiness Group and the Army's new approach to combat readiness. I also knew that Guard commanders in Florida thought the Readiness Group was too pushy and wanted to command their units rather than influence them toward combat readiness.

In light of these factors, I made a guess as to what was wrong. Adding to these dynamics, the normal length of a tour at Patrick was three years, but the current commander had been there only about 18 months; accordingly, Gen. Matheson must have agonized over his decision before he talked to me. I recognized that his decision had probably already been made and that it was final and non-negotiable.

Evaluating all of this in the moment after he posed his question to me, my reply was, "How soon do you want me to go down to Patrick Readiness Group and try my hand at solving the problem – whatever that problem is?" He answered, "I prefer that you go now and take command of the unit."

I dreaded going home that day and breaking the news to the family. They all had hoped to be in the Atlanta area for the next few years. Kent would finish high school in Atlanta in about four and a half months, and Scott would complete the school year within five months. Kent was in the process of considering what college or university he would like to go to.

So, once again, Peggy would have to work with both boys, as neither son was happy about the upcoming change. Because my reassignment was effective immediately, Peggy would have the added strain of selling the house and telling our neighbors that she was once again alone.

I went on to Patrick and planned for the assignment there being at least a three-year tour.

C hapter 25
Patrick Readiness Group

The move to Patrick Air Force Base ended my job in Atlanta as the Infantry Coordinator for Army National Guard and Special Forces units in the southeastern states and Puerto Rico. In the future, I would be dealing with personnel in the Florida National Guard and the Army Reserve units throughout the State of Florida. At the time I arrived, an Air Force colonel was in command of Patrick, which provided housing for the Army Readiness Group.

Patrick Air Force Base is located right on Florida's Atlantic coast in between the Banana River and the coastline. The Banana River separates the base from Merritt Island, the Indian River and the main coast of Melbourne and Cocoa. It is in a beautiful setting blessed with plenty of sunshine and an abundance of blue water – the kind of place that those who live up north in winter dream about, the type of area that Florida's tourism industry is built on. From the Officers' Club and the NCO Club, you could see the rockets on the launch pad just to the north at Kennedy Space Center.

Since much of the NASA operation had been moved to Houston, Texas, plenty of base housing was available. This may have been the reason for the Army Readiness Group being placed on what was an Air Force base.

The Readiness Group was about 75 to 90 personnel strong and was supported by a fleet of automobiles, supplemented by five Army UH-1 helicopters and three fixed-wing, 8-passenger aircraft. Personnel in the Readiness Group were seldom home on the weekends. These separations could have been cause for concern, but once Peggy had moved from Atlanta and gotten settled in at Patrick, she worked closely with the wives and kept that concern in check. An Army wife has *many* unspecified jobs!

My first obligation was to meet the base commander, Colonel Joseph L. Pospisil, who was in the process of retiring from military service after some 30 years. He welcomed me to his Air Force base and provided temporary base quarters. The quarters next door to his were being reserved for us until such time as Peggy and Scott could make the move. Col. Pospisil's replacement, Colonel Joseph McClure, would be arriving soon.

After a very pleasant reception, I met the deputy base commander, Lt. Colonel Walter A. Brocato, who took me under his wing like a long-lost child. He couldn't have been more hospitable, as was his lovely wife, Peggy Anne. Wives are very important in military life.

Then it was time to meet the colonel I was replacing. Colonel Waters and his wife Olivia lived off base and were going to retire in Cocoa, Florida. It wasn't long after our meeting, which was cordial, before he disappeared. He took a vacation until his retirement was official. My orders became effective immediately, but I kept a low profile until he cleared his office.

The Mission

By this time, my mission was clear. The mission of the Readiness Group, which was made up mainly of combat veterans, was to influence the combat preparedness of the National Guard and Army Reserve units in Florida. These highly skilled and seasoned specialists would *influence* the Guard and Reserve units, *but they had neither the capability nor the authority to issue commands to any unit.*

The following branches of the military services were included: Judge Advocate, Adjutant General, Intelligence, Military Police, Medical Service, Quartermaster, Personnel, Finance, Engineers, Chemical, Infantry, Armor, Ordinance, Air-Defense Artillery, Artillery, Signal, and Transportation. In Florida, these types of units for the most part were found either in the Guard or the Reserve.

The chain of command was different for each branch of service. The Army National Guard was commanded by the Adjutant General of Florida, who had authority from the state government except when units were nationalized.

The Army Reserve units in Florida were commanded by Army generals from headquarters in Atlanta. The exception to this command arrangement in the Reserves was the 143rd Transportation Brigade, which was headquartered in Orlando, Florida and commanded by Brigadier General James D. Randall. The unit's next higher headquarters was in Atlanta.

World War II was fought using all branches of service, including the National Guard and Army Reserves, which were mobilized and committed to the war effort. In peacetime, the National Guard and Reserves were accustomed to being activated for emergencies such as hurricanes, floods, fires, earthquakes and civil disturbances.

None of these peacetime uses of military personnel included being committed against a hostile enemy force that had only one thing in mind – namely, they wanted to kill you. This scenario had become a reality, and training for combat was a necessity. Realistic training for preparedness had to be emphasized throughout, particularly by the chain of command.

Fortunately, my year and a half as Infantry Coordinator in several states taught me that there is a tremendous amount of leadership in National Guard officers. The NCOs knew what their job was and could achieve any objective. They may have been referred to as "weekend warriors," but they were dedicated and resilient. The Readiness Group's role was to assist them in their responsibilities as leaders.

My philosophy for training and my interpretation of the mission was explained and expressed in the first meeting and in every subsequent meeting held at the Readiness Group. Mrs. Barbara Metten, my secretary, was always at the "pep talks," as I wanted everyone to relate the objectives of the group in their telephone or written communications.

Soon after my arrival at Patrick, Barbara arranged for me to meet with Brigadier General K. C. Bullard, who was at that time the commander of the Light Infantry Brigade head-quartered in Tampa. The brigade consisted primarily of three infantry battalions and a 105 artillery battalion.

Getting to Know the People

Gen. Bullard was the elected tax collector for Hillsborough County and had his office at the county seat in Tampa, so my visit was with a "weekend warrior." I must say that even though the visit was cordial, I at first felt a sensation like walking into a refrigerator. His experience with the previous Readiness Group leader had not been the best. However, the awards and decorations I wore on my uniform and my combat experience in Vietnam seemed to impress him. This was my intention. It was important that he understood how I planned to lead the Readiness Group, since he was commanding three infantry battalions.

I let him know that I was bringing into the Readiness Group Lt. Col. James Harris, who had been my deputy in the 1st Battalion, 16th Infantry, when I led the battalion in Vietnam, a seasoned combat veteran who might be of use to Gen. Bullard in his quest for combat readiness.

The meeting seemed to go well, and I felt it was a promising start to working with the Guard in that area.

The general invited my wife and me to attend the next National Guard social event in the Tampa area, which included more than just his brigade. Peggy came down from Atlanta for the occasion.

At that gathering, two things happened which helped me to accomplish one of my primary goals for the Readiness Group, which was to elevate the Group's professionalism.

Peggy had graduated from Plant City High School with the commander of a 155 artillery battalion in Sarasota, Lt. Colonel Robert L. Mohler. He was open and frank in his comments to me: "Colonel Ken, I don't care what you do at Patrick, but don't 'toy' with my LTC artillery assistance officer from the Readiness Group. He is the best we ever had." His assistance officer from Patrick was a seasoned combat artillery officer.

The second thing happened when I praised then-Lieutenant Mickey Purchet of the Florida National Guard, who earned the Silver Star for gallantry in action on September 5, 1969 when he was a platoon leader in Charlie Company, 1/16th, in Vietnam. Lt. Purchet would eventually rise to full colonel.

As time went on, Gen. Bullard was promoted to Adjutant General of the Florida National Guard and moved to the headquarters of the Guard in St. Augustine, Florida. This is the only National Guard headquarters that is not collocated with a governor at a state capitol. Gen. Bullard was later promoted to major general and accepted quarters adjacent to those of the Guard.

Gen. Randall worked for 36 years in the school district of Hillsborough County. He had several degrees in education and had also attended some of the Army educational centers. The General James D. Randall Middle School on Fish Hawk Boulevard in Lithia, Florida, was named in his honor.

The path from National Guard headquarters and Patrick Air Force Base became well worn as Gen. Bullard and I developed a close working relationship. My association with Gen. Randall was equally close. I thoroughly enjoyed working with both commanders.

The transportation brigade's headquarters was so close to Patrick Air Force Base that I mostly used our vehicles for coordination. The Readiness Group's air assets were also put to good use.

There were two available training camps. The training facility at Camp Blanding, where the Readiness Group spent a lot of time, is owned by the Florida National Guard. When I taught school in Starke in 1952, I lived close to Blanding, so the area was well known to me.

The other training facility owned by the Army was at Fort Stewart, Georgia. It was used for training by the Guard and Reserve units and was the main training area for artillery units.

I developed a lot of respect for the Guard and Army Reserve personnel during the three years I served at Patrick Air Force Base.

Settling In

By the end of June 1975, Kent had graduated from high school in Atlanta and Scott had finished the tenth grade. Peggy sold the house in Atlanta and made all the other necessary arrangements for the move to Patrick. She also took care of the packing and shipment of furniture. The unpacking went well without me, as usual, and soon everyone was all settled in.

About the time Peggy and the boys settled into quarters at Patrick, the new base commander, Col. Joseph A. McClure, and his wife JerriAnne moved into base quarters next to the one promised to us. Also, Lt. Col. Jim Harris and his wife Doris purchased a house in Satellite Beach. Jim was leader of the Infantry Team at the Readiness Group.

During the time we lived at Patrick Air Force Base, Scott enjoyed surfing on the beach and made many friends at nearby Satellite Beach, where he graduated from high school.

Kent enrolled in Florida Southern College in Lakeland, Florida, where he played soccer and enjoyed his fraternity experiences. He also became very involved with the college's ROTC program. Between his junior and senior years, he qualified as an Army paratrooper and also qualified as an Army Ranger, earning the right to wear a Ranger tab.

A Rocket's Red Flare

Not long after we had settled in, Major General Kendall replaced Gen. Matheson at Readiness Region IV in Atlanta, making Gen. Kendall my immediate boss. My first request was for him to concur in my plans to ask the base commander to authorize officers, NCOs and civilians to conduct a Christmas party at the Officers' Club. He concurred, so the next step was to propose this to Joe McClure. He also concurred, and the planning was on.

A portion of the Officers' Club assigned to the Readiness Group that would be used for the Christmas party was the northernmost ballroom, from which it was possible to see the Kennedy Space Center. When the party was being planned, no one was aware that the Space Center had scheduled the launch of one of their rockets on that particular night.

At around nine o'clock on the evening of the party, the northern sky lit up like a huge roman candle. Everyone gathered by the windows and watched the rocket until it had disappeared from sight. We were all amazed that we had such a perfect spot for viewing the rocket rising through the night sky toward the heavens, adding a special sparkle to the celebration! This party did a great deal for the morale of all personnel assigned to the Army Readiness Group.

C hapter 26
Standing Down

It was in January 1978 that options were presented by Career Management. None of the options appealed to me, so I made the decision to terminate my Army career and move back to my birthplace – Plant City, Florida. My intention to retire was made known to Generals Kendall, Bullard and Randall, and the required paperwork was submitted through channels.

It wasn't long after that process had been started that Peggy hosted a luncheon at home for a visitor. The visitor was the lieutenant general commanding the 1st Army, who made the trip from Maryland to Patrick Air Force Base to tell me that he would be in charge of the next Army Promotion Board. The significance of his visit was not lost on me.

Who knows what might have happened in the future if I had continued my Army career at that point? I knew that I could have stayed in the Army for at least three more years at my current rank of full colonel. Nevertheless, I thanked the three-star general for the information and for his trust in me, but advised him that my decision to retire was final.

The paperwork indicated that 30 June 1978 would be my retirement date. Accordingly, Peggy and I went to Plant City and made arrangements to purchase a house under construction at 1806 North Teakwood Place in the Walden Lake section of the community. We were assured that construction on the house would be finished in time so that we would have a house to move into when we left Patrick.

Gen. Bullard requested that I come to St. Augustine, where I would receive the Florida Distinguished Service Medal, the Governor's award for outstanding and meritorious service. It was dated 22 May 1978 and signed by the Florida Adjutant

General. This event occurred two days prior to the scheduled retirement ceremony at Patrick.

Gen. Kendall came down from Atlanta and conducted the retirement ceremony.

Gen. Randall attended the ceremony, as did Col. David Whitston, my classmate in ROTC at the University of Florida. David and I had been commissioned 2nd lieutenants of infantry on a field just 500 yards from the "Swamp" in Gainesville. Gen. Randall presented a plaque for distinguished service from his headquarters in Atlanta and from his unit, the 143rd Transportation Brigade. Gen. Kendall presented the Army's Legion of Merit and praised the Readiness Group for outstanding service.

Charlotte Walden and Gene and Margaret Sikes from Plant City also came to Patrick for the ceremony, and all guests and the Readiness Group gathered at the Officers' Club for a celebration afterwards. Kent was at jump school at Fort Benning and could not attend.

The food table was decorated with flowers placed in each of my jump boots, which Scott helped Peggy decorate. The table had a wide variety of food loaded with temptations of all kinds (my favorites were on the dessert table!).

We all had fun, and that ended a military career which spanned 32-1/2 years including reserve and active duty.

C hapter 27
Medals and Awards

My military career included both enlisted service and commissioned service. The highest enlisted service rank was corporal. The highest commissioned service rank was full colonel.

Decorations and awards include the following, which were received from various entities and service affiliations:

Silver Star with 1 Oak Leaf Cluster
Legion of Merit with 2 Oak Leaf Clusters
Bronze Star Medal with 2 Oak Leaf Clusters with "V" Device
Purple Heart
Air Medal with 10 Oak Leaf Clusters
Joint Service Commendation Medal
Army Commendation Medal
Asiatic-Pacific Campaign Medal
World War II Victory Medal
Army of Occupation Medal (Japan)
National Defense Service Medal with 1 Oak Leaf Cluster
Vietnam Service Medal with 4 Campaigns
Republic of Vietnam Campaign Ribbon with Device 60
Republic of Vietnam Gallantry Cross with Palm
Vietnam Civil Action Honor Medal (1st Class)
Armed Forces Honor Medal (1st Class) (Vietnam)
Combat Infantry Badge
Parachute Badge
Ranger Tab
Pathfinder Badge
Department of the Army General Staff Identification Badge
Florida Distinguished Service Medal (Governor's Award)

Many of the awards and decorations that I received were earned by the courageous and valiant soldiers it was my honor and privilege to lead in combat in Vietnam: the men of the 1st Battalion, 16th Infantry.

My military career would not have been possible if I had not believed in the following:

> *A scout is trustworthy, loyal, helpful, friendly, courteous, kind, obedient, cheerful, thrifty, brave, clean, and reverent.*

The oath I took was:

> *On my honor, I will do my best to do my duty to God and my country, and to obey the scout law; to help other people at all times; to keep myself physically strong, mentally awake, and morally straight.*

I fully understood and always tried to live up to the scout motto:

> *"Be Prepared"*

C hapter 28
Teaching School at Dover

Our retirement at 1806 Teakwood Place proved to be a most enjoyable period of our lives. It had been a very long time since I had moved away from Plant City after the eighth grade at Mary L. Tomlin Junior High School, and it was wonderful to renew old friendships and make new ones. Attending services at the First United Methodist Church and eating out with our friends were real pleasures.

We had owned a ten-acre orange grove in Dover for several years. By this time, it needed a lot of TLC (tender loving care), which fell to me. Doing the physical work necessary to bring the grove into shape was very rewarding. This job kept me satisfied for several weeks, and I was able to relax completely because I didn't expect to receive new movement orders any day.

We made several trips to Salt Springs in the Ocala National Forest, located about 23 miles northeast of Ocala, Florida. The cabin at Salt Springs was owned jointly between Peggy and her brother, Perry Sparkman. It was a good place to slow down, unwind and let go. The cabin had access to two large lakes where the fishing was good – bass, blue gills, shell crackers, speckled perch, and catfish were found in abundance.

Swimming in the Springs or going boating down the run to Lake George (a fairly wide spot in the St. Johns River) was fun, too, and we found that fishing was good in the run as well. The St. Johns River is one of only a few that flow from south to north. The northernmost mouth of the river ends in Jacksonville, where it opens into the Atlantic Ocean.

That lifestyle was great for a while, but I must admit I was vulnerable to someone offering me a job. As it turned out, however, other matters had to be addressed first. During the first three or four months of retirement, some individual health problems surfaced and it was imperative to take immediate action to address those issues.

The VA

Not only had the doctors at Patrick conducted several physical exams to protect the government against any false claims after retirement, but the Veterans Administration (VA) also conducted their own health investigations. The physicals conducted at Patrick Air Force Base had determined that I had high blood pressure and a weak back, and that both were service-connected.

The physicians at the VA Hospital in Tampa, who conducted their own physicals, concurred that both the high blood pressure and weak back were service-connected. Based on these concurrences, the VA rendered me 10% disabled for hypertension and 10% disabled for a weak back, and designated both as being service-related.

The VA hospital in Tampa set up treatment schedules to insure that the high blood pressure problem would be continually treated, and the weak back problem would also be closely monitored.

There was more. The VA doctor in Tampa determined that I had two other health problems. First, my teeth and gums needed surgery, and this could be performed at the VA headquarters in St. Petersburg. Appointments for the surgery were set up and I followed through on that right away.

The second identified health problem was an enlarged prostate gland. My follow-up questions related to how soon a biopsy could be done to determine for certain the seriousness of that condition. The VA hospital could not conduct a biopsy soon, so I made arrangements for a specialist at Watson Clinic in Lakeland to perform the biopsy immediately. The surgery for the biopsy was performed and the results indicated that even though the prostate was slightly enlarged, there was no cancer and a long life could be expected.

This newly validated veteran status was created by my retirement. As a veteran, I have only high praise for the VA health care system. The men I led in Vietnam have indicated to me that they have received outstanding health care from the VA, particularly their care for those veterans suffering from post-traumatic stress disorder (PTSD).

A New Career

After enjoying retirement for about six months, something happened to change everything once again. I was offered a job at Dover Elementary School. Mr. Willis Peters, principal, wanted me to develop a program of Industrial Arts for the Dover Exceptional Student Center.

I didn't especially anticipate developing a program for students with special needs. My wife was a special education teacher when I married her, but I wasn't sure I could relate to the students.

After talking to Mr. Peters, I sought advice from Mrs. Leslie Morris, the Special Ed Coordinator. If I accepted the job, she would be my immediate boss in the chain of command to Mr. Peters. She was quite convincing. The real challenge, she told me, was to accept the fact that *special needs students react to the same things as other students do – a pat on the back or a kick in the rear. Motivation is the key.* I accepted the job and began immediately to improve the existing shop area.

Goals of the Program

The Dover Industrial Arts Program was designed to be a pre-vocational training program for students 12 to 21 years old, and it would be oriented toward the students' performance. Performance-oriented training is simply a method of teaching which places emphasis on the student's performance rather than on the teacher's performance.

The student learns by performing in a hands-on situation. The woodworking laboratory utilizing wood, tools, equipment, and mass production techniques is used as a vehicle for training individuals for job performance. Although the students do gain some specific woodworking skills, these skills are incidental to the core objectives of the program: developing in students the behavior and attitudes that are acceptable to industry. These behavioral objectives include:

1. Observance of safety rules and acceptable reactions to emergency situations.
2. The ability to follow directions.
3. Acceptable participation as a team member in the production of products good enough to offer for sale.
4. An attention span acceptable to industry.
5. Motivation to achieve individual maximum levels of functioning.
6. Punctuality.
7. Acceptance of responsibility.
8. Reduction or elimination of the "failure syndrome."

Research indicates that most of the trainable special needs students who attempt real employment fail because they cannot cope with these objectives satisfactorily, not because they have failed to learn a specific technical skill. Accordingly, students are trained to be as employable as possible in the various community industries.

DoverCraft Industries

I established the woodworking shop for the program as DoverCraft Industries. Students enrolled in the program became "employees" of DoverCraft and were trained to carry out their work assignments in a manner that would be satisfactory in any commercial enterprise. Real machinery and hand tools common to industry were used in the production process. The students' vocabulary was expanded to include terms acceptable to industry, including:

1. We keep it simple.
2. We make no assumptions or presumptions; we check.
3. We observe safety.
4. We do the assigned job cheerfully.
5. We are proud of DoverCraft products.

6. Form follows function.
7. The boss may not always be right, but he will always be the boss.

Few trainable students possess the ability to select, lay out, construct and finish even token projects without considerable instructor assistance. Students of a particular class — 9 to 14 students on any given day — may be involved in the making of only one specific part of a product. When one class departs the shop, the next class picks up where the other left off, and the production process continues. It is a process that is, by nature, repetitious. This repetition allows the students to realize job satisfaction and achieve success, and this reduces or eliminates the "failure syndrome."

Psychology plays a large part in student productivity. Students take pride in the fact that their efforts produce products that people are willing and anxious to purchase with hard-earned cash. They are also happy when they receive one of each item of production, a practice which I instituted in the program. This improves quality control, since they never know which item of production they will receive for their own, and therefore do their best on everything they handle.

Production items are given names, such as The Ponderosa, The Bonanza, The Corral, or The Bronco, and each product is given a careful inspection before it qualifies for sale by DoverCraft Industries. The idea that diligent, hard work can be satisfying and rewarding makes a lasting impression.

It will be most rewarding when many of the current students become taxpaying citizens of the community. When my students in these classes become productive in our local industrial complex, I will know that my venture into civilian life was worth the challenge.

During the almost three years I taught school in Dover, my boss changed. Mrs. Leslie Morris was promoted and became the leader in a larger school where she would be given greater responsibility. Thus, Mr. Jack McMillan became the new coordinator in Dover. He, as well as Mrs. Morris, were always there to evaluate the program.

They told me that my model of challenging the students to be all that they can be – a concept that I tried in every way I could to teach my students and an ideal that I tried to help them incorporate into their lives – had been noted by the school board and even at higher levels of education, including the Florida State Council for Exceptional Children.

I received great job satisfaction and was happy at Dover. Being a civilian was different from being an Army officer, but I took pride in both.

I also took pride in being associated with the other professional educators in the school. They were trained in their specific fields of endeavor. One real pleasure for me was participating in education conventions with them each year.

Moving On

Then it came time for me to make a decision, one which I faced with many mixed emotions. Mr. "Davvy" Davenport had requested the board of directors of the Florida Strawberry Festival and Hillsborough County Fair to seek a replacement for him as the general manager. He wanted to retire in Plant City.

I had to decide whether to submit my name to be considered as his replacement, which would become effective after a short period of on-the-job training. If accepted for this position, which would entail even greater responsibility than that at the Dover school, employment would commence on September 1, 1981.

The decision was made. I submitted my job application along with several other candidates. My application for the position was accepted, and I left the Dover school on July 1, taking with me a lot of job satisfaction. Achieving success as a civilian educator and becoming a satisfied civilian was something I felt I could be proud of.

C hapter 29
The Florida Strawberry Festival
and Hillsborough County Fair

So what did I know about festival management? Truthfully, not much.

Stepping into the unknown was a challenge, but I did have some confidence that I could succeed because of all the management training received at Army schools. Leading the courageous men of the 1st Battalion, 16th Infantry (Mech), in Vietnam was the greatest responsibility I could have ever had. Any problems that might confront me in this new job were slight in comparison to that experience. So I did feel confident.

1930
Remembering the First Festival

The first festival was staged March 12-15, 1930, the year when the Plant City Lions Club sponsored the first Plant City Strawberry Festival to celebrate the bountiful harvest of the strawberry crop grown by local farmers. The Future Farmers of America sponsored the contest won by the first queen of the festival.

Being chosen as the queen of the Strawberry Festival has always been a goal sought after by competitive girls of the Plant City community, and that has been true since Charlotte Rosenberg won the title in 1930. I know she won it because I witnessed her coronation when I was just 3-1/2 years old and my family took me to the festival. That trip to the first festival, when it was called simply the Plant City Strawberry Festival, is still etched in my mind even after so many years.

If ever there was a need for diversion, it was then. Money was scarce and the entire nation was gripped by the Great Depression. People were looking for ways to turn dark clouds into smiles, and having a festival could make that happen.

Tribune research by Panky Snow and Dave Nickolson revealed the following:

Plant City population: 6,800

Grocery prices at local A&P stores:

sugar (5 lbs):	25 cents
butter (1 lb):	45 cents
lettuce (head):	10 cents
potatoes (10 lbs):	36 cents
soap (3 cakes):	20 cents
golden mustard:	15 cents

Autos:

Chevrolet Phaeton	$495
Dodge Six	$835
Pontiac Big Six	$745

Other Goods:

Simmons bed outfit: $18.66
(bed, springs, mattress)

That was the background and the total sum of what I knew about the Strawberry Festival.

1981
Getting Ready

Technically, I was employed by the festival's board of directors on 1 September 1981. Peggy and I decided to visit some friends, Nelson and Mary Ellen Jones, in Charlotte, Vermont. On 2 September 1981 we all went to the Essex Junction Fair near Burlington. That fair specializes in the enjoyment of maple syrup in every way known to man.

We love maple syrup, but my purpose there was to meet the fair manager and learn all he was willing to share about fair management. He spent the next four hours sharing his ten years of experience as the general manager. I told him I had no experience whatsoever in fair management, so I was most appreciative of his cooperation.

Before we left the fairgrounds to go back to Charlotte, he expressed a desire to come to Florida and attend the Florida Strawberry Festival, and if possible be a concessionaire selling Vermont maple syrup. I assured him that every effort would be made to fulfill his wish at the 1983 festival.

We left Charlotte the next day and headed for the Maryland State Fair. My purpose was the same: to learn about fair management. We were cheerfully greeted by the general manager, who had some fifteen years' experience, and he was most hospitable. He suggested that I consider going to the International Association of Fairs and Expositions (IAFE) in Las Vegas, Nevada. The IAFE is an association that specializes in sharing information on fair management. It meets every year in late November or early December, and is international in scope.

Then, back to Plant City and getting to work. I got to know my new boss, "Davvy" Davenport, the current festival general manager. At that time, the organization encompassed two events and was known as the Florida Strawberry Festival and Hillsborough County Fair. I learned that Mr. Davenport knew a lot about management, as he had retired from being a high level manager with a vacuum cleaner company before coming to Plant City.

Mr. Davenport introduced me to his staff. Patsy Brooks had previously worked for Louise Gibbs, who was manager before Mr. Davenport. At the time we were introduced, I wasn't sure whether Patsy had been told that I had been hired to take Davvy's place after the next festival scheduled for 1982. Carolyn Eady was Davvy's secretary and was in charge of the concessions area. Carolyn had been with the festival for several years also. Both of these ladies had considerable experience in the festival business.

The next staff member was the bookkeeper, Christy Meyer, who was new to the Plant City area. She had gotten a little bit of computer experience elsewhere, and told me it would be nice if the festival could purchase a computer to use. That probably wouldn't happen before the next festival, as I discovered that the festival didn't have much money.

There was one other person on the staff. He was known only as "Junior," and he was in charge of maintenance. The festival had only this one maintenance man and he didn't have even a small office to call his own, much less a shop he could keep his equipment in. The festival owned a mowing machine and a small farm tractor, and these were parked in the yard. Junior and I owned the only two pickup trucks the festival had available, and both were used extensively. My truck was about two years old. I spent $80 per month of my own money just on gasoline.

It wasn't long, however, before Davvy hired a second maintenance person. The new maintenance man, David Corbin, had come to Plant City from the north and had some previous engineering experience. Davvy also arranged with a local contractor named Mr. Joe Merrin to keep the grounds clean when the festival would be running, and the grounds were indeed kept clean because of the professionalism of Joe Merrin.

I received permission from Davvy for Peggy and me to attend the IAFE convention in Las Vegas. The manager in Maryland was right; one could learn a lot from the IAFE attendees, and I needed to learn a lot, fast. The festival was scheduled to begin just two short months from then.

1982
A Learning Experience

Two weeks before the festival opened, Davvy said: "Ken, I want a contract to have two people-movers constructed for moving our patrons from the west parking lot to the entrance at Gate 16. The people-movers will reload at Gate 16 and return to the west parking lot."

This operation was to begin on opening day and continue each day during the nine-day festival. The farm tractor the festival owned wasn't large enough to pull a people-mover so I guessed, correctly, that procurement of such a vehicle was also up to me. I was going to need some help.

From this point on during the next 14 years, I would lean heavily on one of the largest strawberry farmers in the area.

Mr. Roy Parke was the festival president and chairman of the 16-member board of directors and 14 associate directors. Roy was an immigrant who moved to the United States with his family from Ireland when he was eight years old. His dad bought a farm in Pennsylvania, and Roy worked on the farm and went to a one-room schoolhouse there. He was about four or five years older than I was, but much wiser. I decided to consult with him about this project.

Roy and I started with a schematic that I drew up the night before of my vision of what a people-mover should look like, then went over to the state fairgrounds in Tampa to see a people-mover already in operation. Theirs looked something like my diagram, but theirs opened from the rear onto the roadway. We wanted our patrons to exit on the sidewalk side of the street for safety reasons. Roy solved one of my other problems when he assured me that he would provide at least one large farm tractor to pull the people-mover, if we could get it built and operational in just two weeks.

We found just the person to build our people-movers out on State Road 60 near Brandon. The builder assured Roy and me that he would have two people-movers delivered to the festival two days prior to opening day. Painting them would be up to us. Somehow, Roy arranged for one more farm tractor to pull the second people-mover.

Believe it or not, there were two people-movers in operation during the nine days of the 1982 festival. As we found out from experience, however, those two movers were not enough to handle the large crowd of fairgoers. A decision was made to have a total of six movers running for the nine days during the next festival in 1983.

Roy Parke was in my cubbyhole office every day, and we often recounted the previous day's activities. If board action was needed, I let Roy know well ahead of the next board meeting so that he could count his votes early. Then it was Davvy's job to make formal recommendations to the board of directors, and Roy paved the way for Davvy to get quick approval.

Things were now moving rapidly. The grounds took on a vibrant look. Jim Murphy, the midway owner, had moved in and erected all his sideshows and exhibitions. Carolyn Eady was busy getting the concessionaires placed in the proper order on the festival grounds. Then I was faced with another, unexpected challenge. Davvy told me that I would be the stage manager for the country music artists who would be performing their magic on the stage. A semi flatbed truck had been placed in position as a stage for their performances.

As stage manager, all I knew was that there were a lot of lights to go on the stage and a lot of sound equipment. Then Davvy told me it would be nice if I could figure out how to place 1,000 seats in front of the stage. What a surprise! Since the festival grounds doubled as a football field for the high school in Plant City, the field was flanked by concrete bleachers that could seat 3,600. The 1,000 seats Davvy wanted would be in addition to the 3,600 in the concrete bleachers.

Junior and Dave Corbin spent a good part of the night determining how this could be done, and another feat was accomplished: the 1,000 seats in front of the stage were ready for opening day. Some of these seats were reserved for members of the board of directors and their guests. During the festival, the bleachers and the seats were filled to capacity by crowds eager to hear the music and watch their favorite country artists perform.

Davvy planned and had the maintenance crew install the fencing required for crowd control during concerts, and the Hillsborough County Sheriff's Department and the Plant City Police Department provided security.

The country music artists and the festival patrons arrived about the same time. Mostly, I tried to stay out of the way as two shows were performed daily. The thing that saved me as a new stage manager was a volunteer named Mr. Gene Lyons. He had worked stage areas before and led me day by day. He was very familiar with sound and lighting equipment, but most of all he knew how to talk to the artists' road managers. They couldn't push him too far!

On the second day of the festival, I was summoned to the office. Davvy was in trouble. Patrons had swarmed the office complaining about the sheriff's deputies not allowing their family members reentry to the grandstands after some members of the party left to go to the restroom. When patrons attempted to reenter, they were denied admittance by the sheriff's deputy on duty at each end of the stands.

There was a reason this was being done. An agreement between the sheriff and fire department dictated that, for safety reasons, when the 3,600 seats were full, no one else would be allowed to enter.

It became apparent that Davvy had some unhappy patrons. The festival's success depended on happy people, so I devised a plan and arranged for action to be taken that I thought would solve the problem.

I contacted a local printing company with an order to print 3,000 two-inch by three-inch "potty passes" on stiff yellow paper. That was all, just print the word "potty pass." It was 2:30 p.m. at the time I gave my order, and I gave the printer a very strong admonition that the passes had to be delivered to Mr. Davenport, festival manager, not later than 4:30 p.m. that day. At first, the printer resisted the delivery deadline, but I made it clear that his future business with the festival depended on the 4:30 p.m. delivery of the passes.

Well, the 4:30 p.m. deadline for delivery of the 3,000 "potty passes" was met. The passes were given to the sheriff's deputies controlling the grandstand entry points, and they handed out a pass to any patron leaving the stands for whatever reason. The person seeking reentry to the grandstand had to surrender the pass to the sheriff's deputy before going back in.

This incident reinforced what I already knew: if a problem can be properly identified, a solution can be found. Davvy was relieved that I had found a solution to his problem and made the festival patrons happy once again. The "potty pass" was utilized for several years, and may be in use even now for those patrons sitting in the free 3,600-seat grandstand.

Several things became clear after that first festival: country music was in demand by our patrons; crowd control measures had to be an integral part of future planning; and money must be made to insure that we could increase the number of restrooms available on the grounds, especially more for the ladies. It was also clear that an elevated stage must be built with a cover that would protect the entertaining artists and their equipment from rain. It was a fortunate coincidence that we didn't have rain during my first festival.

My experiences in 1982 would prove to be invaluable in planning for future festivals.

Christy Meyer was a key figure in festival operations, since financing was her specialty. She needed a computer, but she also needed more training on how to use it most effectively. Both of these requirements were fulfilled now that we had some money from the 1982 festival.

The 30th of June 1982 finally arrived and, to use military language, a "change of command" ceremony took place. Although it was Davvy's decision to leave and retire, he would be missed. I learned so much from Davvy. It seemed as though he had the ability to see into the festival's future. He made decisions and stood by his convictions.

Now that the 1982 festival is over, where do we go from here?

Planning Ahead for 1983

First of all, I wanted to get the "chain of command" understood by all employees. In the military, training is something that never ceases. It must be continuous. As for me, I must learn to be a civilian leader, but never forget my military training. The chain of command is important because we never know what tomorrow may bring. In combat, if a leader must be replaced, the person filling his slot must carry on with the same knowledge that the replaced person had been taught. Notice that I didn't say the replaced person was killed or wounded, but in reality that could happen, even in civilian life.

The first decision was to name someone who could be responsible in my absence. Patsy Brooks was my choice to be the assistant manager. She would accompany me to every board of directors meeting. This was something new, as she had not been allowed to attend meetings before. She would be given all the responsibility she was capable of handling so that if I had to be away, or if something happened and I was incapacitated, she would know how to take over immediately.

One area in which Patsy was capable of providing leadership was the agricultural arena. Her son Scott had raised pigs and steers. She and Bobby, her husband, had learned a great deal about the field of agriculture from Scott, so that would be her specialty. I would concentrate on the building aspects of the festival's requirements.

Almost immediately, I would be called on to use my industrial arts experience. We would build a stage that would be elevated to at least eight feet high and have rain protection overhead. Scaffolding was envisioned to set 4 x 8-foot sheets of 3/4-inch plywood fastened to 2 x 6-inch treated pine. Glue, screws and bolts would hold the sections of the stage together. This would be a quantum leap improvement over the flatbed trailer.

There were several steps involved in making this happen.

Because this would be a more permanent fixture, a major decision had to be made. Where should this stage be located? Since the sun comes up in the east and sets in the west, logic dictated that it must be erected on the east end of the football field. This way, all the patrons sitting in the concrete bleachers, which faced toward the east end of the field, would have a better view of the performing artist.

You might argue that placing the stage there would require the performing artist to look into the sun during the afternoon show. Exactly true, but they look into the bright stage lights anyway (and perhaps they squint all the way to the bank!). The patron must take priority, and they would be more comfortable looking toward the east during the afternoon show when the sun would be behind them.

Next, I obtained concurrence from Junior and David Corbin. Since they didn't have a shop, all of their construction would be accomplished in the main exhibit building. Now, let them build it, but make no assumptions or presumptions. One must check on the progress.

Then my attention turned to Roy Parke once again. He must concur in the concept, but he needed to count his votes before I made a recommendation to the board. He did his homework and we continued to march after the board approved my recommendation.

During this same time period, in connection with Carolyn Eady's area of responsibility, I fulfilled a promise I had made when I visited the fair in Vermont – I asked Carolyn to find a place for a Vermont maple syrup concessionaire and make arrangements for it happening. This was Carolyn's specialty. She sought out the best concessionaires she could find and planned extensively for where they would be placed on the festival grounds.

Carolyn's requirements for the future would necessitate expansion of the current size of the festival grounds. This expansion was something that would have to be accomplished over time, and it was a venture that would require me to make recommendations to the directors for their approval.

Roy Parke had great vision. He believed there were two areas that could allow for possible expansion and these should be investigated. One possibility was the American Legion building. He said, "Let's buy it – they want to move away from the festival anyway." Count your votes, Roy, and let me know when to make recommendations to the board. The board approved the purchase, and now I could work out the plans for the new stage in detail.

It would go on the east end. There would be 1,000 seats for the directors directly in front of the stage, and behind the directors would be as many chairs as we could procure.

Davvy's 1,000-seat idea taught me that there was a big demand for country music venues at the festival, and satisfying this demand required more seating than just the 3,600 spaces in the concrete bleachers we had available. Carolyn Eady was given the task of finding the cheapest, most durable chairs that we could buy. Even at this point, no one envisioned selling these seats. An offset to the expense would be accomplished by the increase in the number of gate tickets we would sell. The patrons' desire for more country music would take care of how these additional seats would be paid for.

Since we now owned the American Legion building, we could continue to use the building for the free exhibits in the "Neighborhood Village." The directors' desire for a meeting place could also be realized by renovating the upstairs of the American Legion building.

With some help from our maintenance crew, several directors volunteered to help renovate on weekends. Bud Clark, Frank Moore and Roy Parke were three that could be depended on each weekend. This project was completed and the meeting place opened for use during the 1983 festival.

1983
Flying Solo

It was late 1982 and early 1983 that construction was completed on the first increase in the number of restroom facilities. This provided relief to patrons of Jim Murphy's midway and to those in the main exhibit building. That restroom was built near Gate 16.

It was also the year that sewer hookups and electrical connections were provided for Carolyn Eady's concessionaires. The same year, demolition of all buildings on the lot just south of Gate 10 was completed in order to make room for bus parking.

All of these improvements resulted in an increase in revenue collected at the gates and from Jim Murphy's midway.

I started using a small storage room for sleeping quarters on the festival grounds 24 hours per day during each festival. I wanted to be available if needed. Joe Merrin will remember my question to him one morning at one o'clock before opening day. Joe, how does one check the oil in a billy goat? No comment on what was meant!

Several other changes and innovations also occurred in 1983.

I made three major recommendations to Roy Parke, and Roy concurred in all three. He convinced 16 voting directors and their wives to accompany him and Helen to Las Vegas for the IAFE convention. This trip would be beneficial because of the exposure to how other festivals and fairs were operated. Many accepted Roy's offer and enjoyed the trip at festival expense. This exposure and meeting others in the festival-fair business was well worth it. My recommendation to Roy must have been a good one; voting directors are still going to Las Vegas every year and enjoying it!

I also suggested to Roy that every director and associate director be assigned a specific duty, a task to be performed not only during the festival but also throughout the year. That must have been a good recommendation, too, because every director has a job even to this day.

The third recommendation required some tact to achieve. It dealt with the selection of the festival queen and her court, which was a very sensitive issue. I felt that the selection of the festival queen and court should be based on much more than physical beauty. The young ladies should also have the ability to relate to people in a most effective way. They should have the ability to express themselves well before an audience, and they must react to questions posed by their judges. Those chosen should be outstanding representatives for the festival. Today, the contest is conducted in exactly that manner.

This was the year that I gained experience as a talent agent. Roy Parke and Joe Newsome, another director, asked me to book talent in order to save booking fees. Booking talent was not my bag, but I did it for the next three years. The three of us, accompanied by our wives, made the trip to Nashville each year. The Country Music Association knew us well.

Louise Mandrel performed on the newly constructed stage on the east end of the stadium, and her performance for the afternoon show was excellent.

After the show was over, a heavy rain started coming down, and the wind blew the cover off the stage. When the rain and wind ceased, a dry indoor/outdoor carpet was procured by David Corbin and placed on the entire stage, so that it was ready for Louise to perform her second show. The microphone she held was dry and the stage floor was dry. These timely actions prevented her from getting an electrical shock from a wet stage.

David Corbin and his maintenance crew had reacted to a potentially dangerous situation in an exemplary manner. The country artist thanked the festival for making the stage safe for her. Sam Marino, who provided stage lighting, was especially thankful, as was Billy Fitch, who provided the sound.

Gene Lyons continued to be the stage manager and had an excellent rapport with the artists' road managers. Gene was also the individual who provided invaluable assistance in securing bulldozers to clear additional parking lots.

Junior went back north to live, and David Corbin was made supervisor of a maintenance team of three year-round employees.

The 1983 festival was a huge success. Our staff worked hand in glove with each other, and I was extremely proud of them.

1984
A Year of Expansion

Another busy year was in store in 1984 and good things continued to happen for the festival. The Florida National Guard artillery unit had a new armory built for them near the airport. Their move enabled the festival to obtain the old property that was next door to the festival grounds. The gun shed on the vacated armory property was renovated and made into cubicles for concession rentals and was known as the "Carriage House." This made Carolyn Eady happy and put several Plant City contractors to work. The armory building was renovated by Plant City general contractor Clayton Jenkins, who did an excellent job. The renovation was a complete success.

This purchase provided the expansion of the festival grounds that had been needed. The festival now owned about 32 acres and was continuing to increase in size and facilities. The exact dates will not be placed on the expansion, which occurred over several years' time, but could be determined by an evaluation of the aerial photographs taken each year beginning in 1983.

The photographs were obtained through the courtesy of Carlos Videl, a local Plant City businessman and aerial photographer. Carlos was another immigrant, like Roy Parke, but he had come to Plant City from Cuba about the time Fidel Castro came into power. Carlos and his wife were special friends who lived nearby and had looked after Peggy when I was in Vietnam. The Videls had several children, all of whom graduated from Plant City High School and then trained overseas to be a part of the family business.

David Corbin needed a shop and equipment to increase maintenance productivity. Through necessity, because of the acquired buildings and land area, his responsibilities also had expanded over the years. A nearby church decided to relocate and when their old property came up for sale, the festival bought it. David renovated the building himself and established a permanent maintenance shop, conveniently located on State Road 574 near the festival grounds.

The festival purchased several acres of land which abutted State Road 92 on its south side that was owned by a Plant City lawyer, Mr. Trinkle. This provided a large parking lot for use by the festival. The overrun of midway vehicles was housed on part of the lot, and 20 spaces were used for an RV parking lot. It had sewer, water and electrical connections.

It was not unusual for those renting the lot to stay for the entire time the festival was open. Patrons would ride the people-movers back and forth to Gate 16. They ate a lot of strawberry shortcake and bought tickets to every country music show.

Many nearby houses were either moved or demolished after purchase of the lots they were on. Jim Murphy's area of operation on an expanded midway was accomplished and made the midway as large as any in the southeastern United States.

Meeting old Friends

A pleasant surprise came during one festival when Thomas Jefferson Frayne and his wife Mary drove their recreational vehicle into our RV parking lot. They were here to spend three days with us, eating shortcake and enjoying the country music shows each day.

Jeff was a classmate at Gulf High School in New Port Richey, but I had not seen him since we were in the Army Air Corps during WWII. He had been stationed in Okinawa and came to Japan to visit me when I was there, and we had dinner together in Tokyo.

When Jeff returned to Florida from Okinawa, he again became a civilian and put down roots in Tampa. It was there that he and Mary founded Frayne's Sportswear Manufacturing, Inc. Jeff will quickly tell you that he was the strong captain at the helm. That is believable, as he led his family through a 33-year climb to netting 15 million dollars in annual clothing sales with 36 stores.

He was the creator of Frayne Sportswear. His designs of casual wear for the mature woman aged 40 and up and his manufacturing skills in making those clothes were well known. His company's manufacturing business was located in West Tampa and occupied 54,000 square feet.

Jeff lived the American dream, and I was privileged to be a part of his graduating class in New Port Richey's Gulf High School, a class of 13 students.

During most of Jeff's exceptional rise in the design, manufacture and sale of clothing, I was traveling all over the world pursuing a military career.

As we talked at the Strawberry Festival, we were reminded of that voyage we had made to "Honeymoon" Island from New Port Richey in the sailboat that Jeff designed when he was 12 years old. Jeff, Dale Swartsel and I were almost carried away by mosquitoes on that trip when Jeff and I were seniors at Gulf High School.

He has eleven other sailboats now, and not one is for sale. Jeff says that he runs all his business as he is sailing and avows, "*I follow the wind.*" Jeff and Mary had eight children. All were involved in the business.

Setting The Stage

There are at least one or more festival directors, like Jeff, who never went to college but who have attained exceptional success in business through their personal drive, determination, and that almost indefinable something – I believe it's called *leadership* – but it's leadership of the highest order.

When Bud Clark was president of the festival, we developed a plan to build bleachers on the north and west sides of the field. This would make U-shaped seating facing east toward the stage so that all patrons would be facing away from the afternoon sun. That way, even the chair seats in the center portion could be used. This plan and the cost figures were presented to the board of directors, but the recommendation failed to pass. This was one of the few recommendations I made to the board that was rejected.

As I recall, the next year I was directed to prepare plans and recommendations for a huge covered stage to be built on the *north* side of the field. Contracts were prepared and construction began. It was finished in February 1991.

The new arena for the country music shows had a fairly serious flaw. The grounds needed flood control to eliminate accumulated water during heavy rains. A flood control plan was devised and contracts let. Huge concrete pipes were installed in front of the stage to flow the water down to the marshland to the west. When the flood area was under control, the west end of the arena was built up with several feet of fill dirt. Now the patrons could look down on the stage rather than up. The newly developed area was connected to ground level by ramps that met the Americans With Disability Act specifications, a one-inch rise for every lineal foot of elevation.

The steel bleachers on the north side of the field had to be moved, and these were shifted over to the west side. The high school now had their own football stadium and there would be no possibility of conflicts between the festival dates and their games. Carolyn Eady was once again ordering folding seats, and these could be conveniently stored under the new stage.

While these projects were going on, we were also busy constructing other buildings and obtaining new equipment that added convenience to the operation and enhanced the attractions at the festival.

I believe it was Jim Redman who wanted a ticket office to be built on a city street on the north side of the grounds. David Corbin's crew built it, not in the main exhibit building as in past years, but in his own maintenance shop, and we started selling reserved seat tickets to the country music shows the same year. It became a great success story.

Patsy Brooks' agricultural area received enormous rented tents for the swine and steer exhibitions. She made it possible for the local students who raised them to take a lot of money to the bank from the sale of these animals.

Many more rental tents were used on the grounds. Free entertainment was provided in some of the rented tents along with tents used to house concessionaires.

At least four to eight new restrooms were built by local contractors, and were connected to Plant City's sewer system.

The last project attempted was a huge steel bleacher on the east side of the arena. A local contractor named Freddy Roach was hired to supervise its construction by a Tampa firm. He did an excellent job. Now the 14,000 seating capacity was realized for patrons to view the country shows presented on the main stage for the evening events. The eastern bleachers were seldom sold for the afternoon show because the patrons had to look directly into the sun.

Dennis Lee

The one entertainer who contributed so much for the enjoyment of our patrons was Mr. Dennis Lee, who was born in Memphis, Tennessee. Both Dennis and his two sisters grew up in an orphanage in Memphis. His goal was to sing and entertain as well as Elvis Presley, who also grew up in Memphis. Dennis started performing at the festival as a mime. He provided entertainment between the afternoon and evening country music shows, mostly in the 3,600-seat stadium.

Dennis sang both our national anthem and the Canadian national anthem at the opening of every IAFE convention at Las Vegas. On one of the return trips from Vegas to Plant City, he asked me to let him perform in one of the big tents covering an entertainment stage.

The rest is history – he has performed three shows a day at every festival in every year since. He has become an icon, with 29 years performing at the festival under his belt.

Roy Parke

What "kind of guy" was Roy Parke? Well, he farmed with his dad in Pennsylvania and was successful. Because Roy was about six years older than I was, he was eligible for the draft during WWII. He entered the Army and was stationed at Warner Robbins Air Corps Airfield near Macon, Georgia.

His commander sent him to St. Louis, Illinois for special training, where he met Helen. They fell in love before Roy had to return to duty in Georgia. Helen traveled by train from St. Louis to Georgia and soon after her arrival there, they were married at the Bibb County courthouse in Macon. Roy was made a citizen of the United States by the judge at that same courthouse. After training, he was sent overseas and fought the Germans as an infantry sergeant. Upon his return from service, he saw his daughter Cheryl for the first time.

Several years later they bought a 10-acre strawberry farm in Dover, and his story, too, is part of the history of Plant City and Hillsborough County. Over the years, Roy and Helen had a total of five children. The whole family has been a great supporter of the festival.

During Roy Parke's two years as Festival president, he did a lot more than attend meetings and vote with the board of directors. One of the things he did boosted not only the festival, but was a boon to every strawberry farmer in the area. As a direct result of his efforts, one could always see the Channel 13 television station (WTVT) promoting the festival through a staff media representative. Channel 13 would send a reporter to cover the news in Plant City, because it is known as the Winter Strawberry Capital of the World.

One year, the reporter sent by WTVT to cover the news came to Roy's farm during a freeze that threatened the crop. Roy set up the specific areas next to his house for the cameras to record temperatures and wind velocity indicators. The reporter, who was not a native to the area, came in high heels and a pretty business suit! While broadcasting in front of a watered strawberry field, with the temperature at 30 degrees or lower, the high heels sank into the mud and almost froze to the spot.

After the broadcast, Roy took the reporter inside his house. Helen provided a coat, and Roy provided some form of liquid for warmth. Roy really knew how to engage the news media and the patrons on the tour buses, both at his coolers and at his produce market on Highway 92. Strawberry shortcake is the market's specialty, and the market is so busy at times that local policemen have assisted in directing traffic. The tour bus patrons looked forward to stopping there, and the festival's promotional advertisements were always in plain view.

Regardless of who was festival president, Roy Parke never stopped supporting the community, but continued doing so by his actions and advertisements.

Other directors also made some significant leadership contributions during their terms as directors. Including Roy, their names are: R.E. (Roy) Parke, B.M. (Mac) Smith, J. Albert (Jake) Miles, Jr., James L. Redman, M.P. (Bud) Clark, William (Billy) Vernon, A.L. (Al) Berry, and Joe E. Newsome.

During my 14-year tenure, the directors were responsible for the acreage the festival owned increasing to about 76 acres.

Some of the People

During the years that I managed the festival, I became acquainted with Mrs. Everidge, who raised her family in a home that was adjacent to festival property. One of her three sons, Cecil, lived next door to us on North Teakwood Place. Mrs. Everidge was living alone at the time and, being so close, was subjected to all the noise of the festival. She never complained, but I made sure she was well taken care of.

The grounds expansion required, to a great extent, the professionalism of Mr. Harold Leslie, who was contracted to demolish many of the existing buildings the festival acquired over the years. Several entrance gates and information booths were constructed during my years managing the festival.

New buildings and all of the old ones needed the attention of a master electrician named Mr. Phillips, who owned Ampro Electric. He and his two sons worked tirelessly on every festival.

The number of restrooms was expanded to over 50, including those built or renovated in the midway area. The expansion was made possible, in large part, by a professional plumber named Lloyd Hart, who owned Amax Plumbing in Plant City. There were few years that he didn't have a new restroom ready for the next year. Service personnel, volunteers from the town of Yalaha, Florida, were placed in all restrooms to insure cleanliness and provide a measure of security. They were not paid for this service, but patrons provided generous tips to show their appreciation.

Special thanks go to Dr. and Mrs. John Verner and Mr. and Mrs. Edward Verner. Both have contributed so much to Plant City and the archives, and also to America's veterans.

Mrs. Susie Gardener Dickens provided the leadership for the Junior Royalty competition. Both Susie and her mother, Mrs. Dickens, deserve a lot of credit for their contributions to the most successful Junior Royal shows.

1991 - Desert Storm

As it sometimes happens, events occurred on the world stage during the time I was working at the festival that had an impact on our nation, and they might have affected my own future as well had things been different. However, the *Desert Storm* ground war against Iraq was initiated, conducted, and successfully ended only 100 hours after it began. President Bush announced the liberation of Kuwait on 27 February 1991.

I was willing to go to this war and again serve my country, but my Army HQ told me that after all the women and children had been deployed, I would be called next. *You are too old, Ken!*

Looking Back

By about 1988 the festival drew patrons in excess of 70,000 per day, and it had become an 11-day event. Today, it still draws over 70,000 visitors or more every day and often has crowds numbering up to 100,000 on weekends. In 1995, the last year I managed the festival, big-name entertainment stars were still on the schedule; that year we had Wayne Newton, Kathy Mattea and Billy Ray Cyrus, as well as Pam Tillis, who was born in Plant City.

Looking back on the success of the festival, I felt that I had contributed to that achievement and thus made a success of civilian life. I was glad that the part of the festival's name which included the word "fair" had been deleted and abandoned. Through my efforts and the separation of the Florida State Fair from the Strawberry Festival, the selection of a queen for the festival would never be challenged again. The practice began with Charlotte Rosenberg in 1930, and the tradition now would be continued each year because the queen would be selected only from the Plant City community, not the entire Hillsborough County area.

Thus ended my festival venture as a civilian.

It had been a good decision to go back to my home town of Plant City. It was where my core values for life were established as a member of Boy Scout Troop Four. That's where I learned about a way of living: the scout law, motto and oath.

Ken Cassels
Manager, Strawberry Festival
Plant City, Florida 1981-1995 (14 years)

C hapter 30
Transitions

The festival endeavor, I felt, had been a success and the festival would be left fiscally sound. My home town could be proud of its achievements from 1930 through 1995. I hoped that my part in all those achievements would be looked on with favor. Well, it was time to move on.

When I was eleven years old, my family rented a cabin for two weeks very close to the actual spring at Salt Springs, Florida. Every day of the two-week vacation, I enjoyed the 72-degree temperature of the clear, cold water gushing out of the ground. Learning to swim well was an everyday goal for me.

It was those two weeks that convinced me that if I were ever successful enough to retire, I wanted to return to Salt Springs. So, now that retirement was at hand, I could do just that. The retirement date was set for 30 April 1995.

In the Interim

Just two years after retirement, while still living in Plant City, the Retired Officers Association at MacDill Air Force Base asked me to brief the Association on the festival. Their account of the briefing is recounted below.

From Jungle Colonel to Festival General

Bullets and strawberries are the career extremes for an infantry colonel turned general manager of the annual Florida Strawberry Festival. On Thursday, March 13, we are not only together to enjoy a good luncheon but we have a speaker who is a retiree and also has successfully followed a new path after active duty with the U.S. Army.

"The festival is very challenging," said Kenneth G. Cassels, Manager Emeritus of the Florida Strawberry Festival and Plant City native, who retired as a United States Army Infantry Colonel in 1978. "The Vietnam War was a challenge and I think our troops met it very well," said Colonel Cassels, who spent a year in Vietnamese jungles – six months leading a mechanized combat infantry battalion. It was a half-year of life-and-death responsibility for hundreds of soldiers.

It's also half a world and years away from patrolling 75 tons of strawberries, 25 tons of whipped cream swirled into shortcake, and serving hundreds of thousands of festival visitors. The berry fest is no mortal firefight for Colonel Cassels, and a year of soldiering in jungles near the Cambodian border was clearly no Sunday picnic. Both required organization, management and leadership skills. From armored personnel carriers to the business desk, the job had to get done and the colonel says he knew the key.

"It sounds trite, but "be all that you can be." Push life as much as you can. If you want to be a festival manager, be the best you can be," said Cassels, who credits his management skills and survival to the U.S. Army.

"I am here because of the American soldier," said Colonel Cassels. "He's the best because he is allowed to use his own initiative to carry out his orders. The North Vietnamese were good. Our people were better. There is no better soldier in the world than the American soldier," said Colonel Cassels, who also thinks the strawberry festival is in a class of its own.

"We probably have the best bargain in the United States. All we try to do is have satisfied customers, and if we do that, then the numbers take care of themselves."

Recent festivals have attracted nearly one million

visitors in ten days. There were 250,000 servings of strawberry shortcake, 40,000 flats of fresh strawberries, 140 tour buses in one day, and thousands of people per sitting at daily concerts. Under the leadership of Ken Cassels the number of visitors doubled in six years.

By comparison, in 1969 Colonel Cassels was responsible for 800 to 1500 men spending 365 days in enemy territory, often as far as 75 miles north of Saigon. He spent 19 years training for a year under fire including day-long battles. "When engaged in combat, you think about what's around you. Our job was to win battles," he said. "We won many battles. You react. That's how you learn to live – get more firepower on them than they had on you. It was the final exam. It was professional soldiering."

Trading bullets for strawberries after 32 years in uniform wasn't that difficult, according to Cassels. "I just came home to Plant City and the festival job 'fit like a glove.' It was the same military principles, contingency plans and deployment, every year; like the Army, our methods did not stifle initiative."

Ken Cassels wasn't promoted directly from Colonel of the jungle to general of the festival. He spent several years in the Pentagon, developing Army policy and helping the military change from a draft-dependent force to an all-volunteer force supplemented by the National Guard and Reserves.

After retiring, he spent two years teaching industrial arts to exceptional students before working on the festivals.

"He's a great guy and does an outstanding job," said one of Plant City's leading lawyers and former president of the Florida Strawberry Festival board of directors. "He's a credit to the community and really a first class good man."

I feel that managing the festival did indeed fit me "like a glove."

Lake Kerr

Now to sell the house in Plant City and find a spot to build a new house on Lake Kerr, one of the most pristine lakes in the Ocala National Forest and in all of Florida. After all, we had been going to Salt Springs on weekends ever since Peggy and I were married and it felt to us like a home-away-from-home. Now it would be permanent.

Peggy found the spot and we bought it. The house in Plant City was sold, and Peggy designed our new house on the purchased property, located about 24 miles from Ocala. The 8-foot elevation of the land provided a 170-degree view of the beautiful lake. The property had 1.78 acres which abutted one of the paved roads.

The sale of our Plant City home was contingent upon the prospective buyer selling theirs. Since we expected there would be some delay selling the house in Walden Lake, a 24 x 36-foot building was constructed so that we could store our furniture. "Beep" Blanchard, a neighbor in Eureka, built it. He knew every phase of building construction, and I enjoyed working with him.

Peggy engaged John Underwood to construct our retirement home on the lake. The day he finished, the house in Plant City sold. Now we could have a house-to-house move, and storage of furniture was not necessary. This was a windfall for me, as now I could use the large 24 x 36-foot building as a workshop in which to construct wooden toys as a hobby.

This marked 17 times that Peggy had to move to support my career as both a soldier and a civilian.

The house and shop in Salt Springs were ready for occupancy on 30 January 1998. The sale of our former home and the transporting of our furniture to the new home were accomplished about the same time.

Now to meet new friends and enjoy retirement again.

Ken and Peggy Cassels
on the dock at their house on Lake Kerr

On Lake Kerr

C hapter 31
Life in Salt Springs

Lake Kerr is connected to a smaller lake by a canal. The smaller lake is known as "Little Lake Kerr." We had owned a small cabin on Little Lake Kerr since 1986. This cabin was next to Peggy's brother's cabin, which also had access to Little Lake Kerr and the canal. We lived in it while Peggy designed and built our retirement home.

The retirement home has been such a pleasure. We could swim in the lake or fish off the dock, which was 6 feet wide and 162 feet long. We could invite friends over to join us in swimming, fishing off the dock, or going for a ride on the pontoon boat to see the sights in and around the lake at a leisurely pace. Having worked hard for over 50 years as a soldier and as a civilian, it made the effort seem very worthwhile.

At the time of the move from Plant City in January 1998, I was about 71 years old. Peggy was about four years younger.

Invitation to a Reunion

In August 2001, we were contacted by one of the rifle companies that I led in Vietnam, Company C, 1/16th Infantry – Bandido Charlie. The Bandidos were planning to have a reunion in conjunction with the reunion being hosted by the Big Red One (BRO) in New Orleans in May of the following year. They invited us to attend and be a part of it. Peggy and I had conflicts with the dates, so we sent regrets, but promised to join them at a later BRO reunion in Reno, Nevada.

9/11

On 11 September 2001, just one month after we received the invitation to attend the reunion, each of the twin towers of the World Trade Center in New York was hit by a large commercial aircraft. The destruction of both of the towers was complete and total.

That same day, shortly after the towers had been hit and were collapsing, another large commercial aircraft slammed into the Pentagon. The Pentagon suffered a great deal of damage, but was not totally destroyed as the World Trade Center was. A fourth large commercial aircraft that had been diverted from its normal flight path and pointed toward a strategic target, believed to be the White House or one of the other capitol buildings, failed in its mission because passengers on board wrested control of the plane away from the hijackers. The plane crashed in a field in rural Pennsylvania.

There were no survivors on any of the four aircraft.

Altogether, over 3,000 people lost their lives in these four attacks, all of which were terrorist motivated. The hijackers were from Afghanistan or originally from Saudi Arabia.

President George W. Bush took immediate steps to launch attacks against Afghanistan to kill Osama Bin Laden, the leader of the terrorists responsible for the attacks against the United States.

Later, President Bush launched attacks against Saddam Hussein, who had murdered thousands of his own Iraqi citizens with chemical weapons of mass destruction and who, it was believed, was also harboring and training terrorists with the aim of sponsoring more attacks against America. Intelligence reports indicated he was again building an arsenal that would inflict massive casualties.

The United States was once again at war.

Honorary Bandidos
2003

The following year, in August 2003, Peggy and I went to Reno, Nevada to join the Bandidos' reunion. Since I was responsible for leading them against the NVA regulars on 12 August 1969, I didn't know whether they would want to thank me or shoot me!

My reservations about their welcome turned out to be unfounded, and the reunion was simply great. It gave me a chance to meet the men for the first time following the change of command in Vietnam. Captain Greenwell, Captain Olson and Captain Ernest L. Freeman were my closest associates there, and Master Sergeant Stephen Rabourn knew many of the NCOs and privates. My friend, the late Major James Harris, who had been Battalion XO for Operations, was represented at the reunion by his wife Doris.

It was Charlie Company personnel – the Bandido Charlies – who were responsible for getting about 30 men from the 1/16th Infantry Battalion of the BRO together, mostly by using the internet. Their efforts have been continuous in expanding the reunions to include Alfa and Bravo Companies.

The first year in Reno, I was asked to speak and tell the wives about Vietnam. I built a replica of the Armored Personnel Carrier (APC) in my shop to help explain some of our experiences. The guys and gals honored Peggy by sharing her birthday cake procured from the restaurant. Peggy and I were pleased and quite enjoyed being honorary Bandido Charlies.

Interviews

The Veterans Administration advised me to get the men to talk. Some, perhaps many of them had not talked even to their wives about their experiences with the enemy in Vietnam. I confess that I was among those who had not done so. These brave men would talk feely to me, since I had the same experiences. My recording machine was busy throughout the reunion, and I conducted five interviews.

I interviewed First Sergeant Alfredo Herrera, Spc. Ron Mackedanz, Pfc. Douglas J. Ludlow, Herbert McHenry and Don Lane. Hopefully, these interviews helped anyone suffering from PTSD.

The first two Bandidos interviewed, Don Lane and Herb McHenry, were members of the platoon that participated in the 10 August 1969 air assault and capture of four soldiers of the 272nd Regiment, 9th NVA Division.

The four NVA prisoners captured in close combat "sang like turkeys" when interrogated by the South Vietnamese. They gave us specific information as to location, size, and weapons of the enemy force. This made us aware that we should expect a much larger force than the one that had been engaged on 10 August 1969, and that we would encounter the enemy between An Loc and the Cambodian border. The intelligence gathered was invaluable. Besides the capture of these enemy combatants, the unit was also credited with killing 23 NVA soldiers in the fight. Their leader was Lt. George Perabo.

Two days later on 12 August 1969, Lt. Perabo was severely wounded and, after ordering Herbert McHenry to continue the attack, stayed behind the rest of the platoon. Doug Ludlow later found him and called for medics to treat and evacuate him. If Ludlow and his men had not found Lt. Perabo, he may have become a prisoner of war or been killed by the NVA forces.

Reunions

After the reunion we missed in 2002, Peggy and I did not miss any 1st Infantry Division reunion until 2010. The first we attended was in Reno, Nevada in 2003, followed by Chicago, Illinois 2004; Phoenix, Arizona 2005; Washington, D.C. 2006; St. Louis, Missouri 2007; Colorado Springs, Colorado 2008; and Dearborn, Michigan 2009. We were looking forward to the next one at San Antonio, Texas in August 2010, but we were unable to attend.

We have also become acquainted with many members of the Bandido Charlie Association at these reunions. I was not a member of Charlie Company, but Peggy and I have been privileged to become honorary members.

The association has graciously invited many to be honorary members. At the risk of accidentally leaving someone out, others we have gotten to know, regular members and honorary alike, are listed here: Rod Tokubo, Sherwood Goldberg, Ed Wallace, Bob Good, Gil Thompson, Joe Calhoun, Mike Renshaw, Phil Arnold, John Finnell, Rufus Hood, Gene Herrera, Bob Schoenwald, Quincy Aulusio, Wayne Parrish, Chester Jahn, Luis Landin, Lonnie Moore, David Sterling, Pat Sullivan, Steve Biernacki, Roger Haynie, and Dawin ("Buddy") Gault.

We also have met many of their family members who have attended the reunions. Michael T. Askew, a medic who served in Alfa Company, has never attended a reunion, but I have talked with him many times by telephone, and I have also gotten to know Dale T. Sunbakken of Alfa Company and Cliff Poris. I interviewed Captain Kenneth J. Costich, commander of Charlie Company just before Phil Greenwell took over.

Ken and Peggy Cassels
2005

"C" Company - Bandido Charlie
1st Battalion, 16th Infantry (Mech)
BRO 1969-70

Down Home

Now back to retirement. Over time, I manufactured 2,000 wooden children's toys in the shop. The power tools were adequate for the job. Some finished products were sold, but I received the most enjoyment from giving them to children who took delight in playing with them. It was the happy look on their faces that brought me such great satisfaction.

Peggy loved to grow things, and grew about 150 azaleas. Her favorite flowers were the ones that require protection from freezing weather – the orchids. These are quite delicate and need special care. Since north central Florida can sometimes have extended periods of freezing temperatures, her care of these beautiful flowers in the winter months is essential.

Peggy's greatest pleasure was fishing in the Ocklawaha River. I went along for the ride and occasionally cut the spikes off her catfish. She and I both enjoyed netting the blue crab, and we also had fun trapping them. Peggy doesn't mind cooking the fish and crabs, as long as I do all the *cleaning*!

Salt Springs does not have a First United Methodist Church, so each Sunday we journeyed the 23 miles to the one on Silver Springs Boulevard (Route 40) in Ocala.

The Forest
and the People of Salt Springs

Perhaps the greatest pleasure of living in Salt Springs is the "laid back" atmosphere of the Ocala National Forest with all its deer, turkey, bear, 'possum, raccoons, and squirrels. Bobcat, coyote and other wild animals have been spotted crossing highways, too.

We also take pleasure in watching the wild birds. Ducks, geese, ibis, blue and white heron, sand hill cranes, and others are some of the many species that are either native to the area or frequently visit the surrounding forest.

Salt Springs could be described as a quaint, small village or town. In spite of its size, however, it has attracted professionals who have built some commercial enterprises there that rival those of larger cities, making it unnecessary to travel any farther than "downtown" to obtain daily necessities. Entertainment isn't hard to find, either, and the citizens have established several social clubs. Impromptu gatherings for food and fun are common.

The people of the community contribute their unique talents and personalities to the place they call home.

The town has one grocery store and two gas pumps owned by Braxton Jones, and there is one other gas station and two restaurants.

The largest restaurant is owned by J. L. and Michele Snowden and their son Jarrett. Kevin Simpson also works at "Bass Champions" as part of the family. Their prime rib dinners on Friday and Saturday nights have been acclaimed the best in Marion County, and their seafood entrees rival those touted by a large national chain. The vegetables taste fresh and are very good. Other specialties include baby back ribs, oysters and oyster stew. They help advertise the Florida Strawberry Festival in season, and they go there every year (I *prompt* them to do so).

Besides working hard in the restaurant, J. L. and Michele both enjoy doing things for the community. To mention just a few examples of this, they participate in various community projects and also sponsor fishing tournaments for the local kids at their back-door pond. Each year, they sponsor lighting spectaculars on Lake Kerr.

The other restaurant is called "The Square Meal," which was started by a family from Elfers, Florida and Memphis, Tennessee. Joe Massey and Jonie had one daughter named Amber. Joe and Jonie operated the restaurant for over 20 years and it was affectionately known as "the gathering place." It has many regular customers for breakfast and lunch, opening at 6:00 a.m. and closing at 2:00 p.m. daily. Bill Barnes and the late Sebert Fowler never missed a meal. Bill is retired from the state and Sebert was a writer and historian.

Joe Massey also became a real estate agent, sharing office space with Jim and Pat Katchie. Pat and Joe ran Advantage Real Estate out of one part of the office, and Jim operated a bait and tackle shop out of the other side. Later, Joe sold the business to Cindy Neuburn, who had three girls and one boy. "Gator," the oldest girl, graduated from the University of Florida and specialized in forestry.

To give you some indication of the relative size of our surroundings, the post office at Salt Springs shares the zip code of 32134 with Fort McCoy, another little town nearby.

Next to the post office is an automatic laundry facility.

The Forestry Service station provides a history of the Ocala National Forest and Salt Springs as well as displays of stuffed animals and reptiles common in the forest.

Another store known as "Buck & Bass" specializes in items for the hunters and fishermen. William Patterson ("Pat") Needham and his wife Dona own the store and have many things for sale manufactured by local craftsmen living here in Salt Springs.

During the winter months in particular, the "snowbirds" flock to Salt Springs to enjoy the milder weather. Besides using Salt Springs as a base camp or jumping-off point for visiting Florida's other places of interest, they seem to like interacting with the natives, sharing their experiences and adding their own personalities to the mix. They don't need to travel very far afield to find amenities.

Hair Solutions for Ladies & Gents on Highway 19 is our beauty salon, previously owned by Diane Burkhalter. When Diane owned the salon, she also worked there as a hair stylist, as did Valerie Howsare and Darlene DuBose. Wallace Griggs was the salon's barber, Karen Cangelosi was a nail technician, and Tina Kincaid was an esthetician. When Mike Howsare and Wally DuBose (Valerie and Darlene's husbands) came in, they would "volunteer" to make coffee and also liked to provide conversation and entertainment for patrons. Diane's sister, Mary Jones of Ocala, is helping me type my autobiography. There have been many changes over time, of course, with some people leaving and new ones taking their places.

Diane and David Burkhalter, her husband, are very community oriented. David loves country music and in the past was lead singer in his professional band called "David Burkhalter and the Wilkinson Brothers," which played locally and nationally. Years ago, he and another band he formed called the "StraightShooters" won a national competition. David enjoys having friends over to play music with him, often inviting the community to bring a dish on special days to enjoy the "pickin' and strummin'." He can be found playing for the local VFW many weekends and at the Valentine's Day dance.

Occasionally, George Custer – who can "tear up" a fiddle playing the Orange Blossom Special – is invited to join them. George, nationally recognized as a Master Fiddler, is a former player with his uncle's band, Georgia Slim and the Texas Round-Up, and also played with Ray Price and other well-known country music stars. In the 1980s, he opened shows for Johnny Cash and Tanya Tucker.

Salt Springs has a great hardware store where you can usually find whatever you need. If they don't have it, they will get it for you. Tools, lumber, paint and plumbing materials are readily available. It is owned by Walt Seiler and his sons, T. C. and Teddy Seiler, who are always friendly and helpful.

"Cactus" Jack was born Albert Jackson Anderson in 1925 in Lake Wales, Florida. He joined the military in 1943 and was an infantry leader in Germany during WWII. During his service he was given Campaign Stars for Normandy and Northern France, a Combat Infantry Badge, and a Presidential Citation for outstanding performance against the enemy. He was injured in September 1944 in Brest, Brittany, and served the remainder of the war in the Transportation Corps near Norwich, England. When he became a civilian, he established "Cactus Jack's" as a place where the local folks could enjoy dancing and drinking "sasparilla." He hosted community events as benefits for sick people or for people who simply needed help with something, and he sponsored an annual chili cook-off where amateur chefs tested their skills. He also was friends with Mel Tillis, the country music singer who now has a home in Lynn, and Mel could be seen there occasionally. Jack died a few short years ago, and his son and daughter took over the business.

The Veterans of Foreign Wars established a post here and have a large hall for food and entertainment. If you are a member, you can enjoy the spirits and food. There are special nights where they may have fish frys or serve steaks, pizza, tacos and taco salads, as well as other food specialties. The AmVets and their ladies also share the hall for flea markets, and the proceeds provide scholarships for local students seeking higher education.

Having enjoyed living in Salt Springs so much, it would be hard not to talk about some of the other people I have met and known who have made living here such a pleasure. Some of them are mentioned here.

Frank M. Lucius taught my granddaughter Martha water skiing. He lives across on the east side of Lake Kerr. Maxie and Jackie McHaffey make excellent knives and once owned the Coors beer distributorship in this area. Ellis Kirkland is a true Christian and now a book writer; before that, he was a master plumber in the Orlando area. Cora Hayes is a seamstress who lives with her husband and daughter in Salt Springs.

Joe Harrison owns a building supply house for builders, "Stuff & Such." He owns several originals from Bill Wessling, the famous artist who paints wildlife scenes. Barry and Portia Ledoux live on Little Lake Kerr. Portia works at Clay Electric, which supplies the area's electricity. Marvin Mullins lives on the banks of the St. Johns River in a house he built near the Fort Gates Ferry, seven miles east of Salt Springs.

Captain Wayne King, who retired from the Fish and Game Commission, lives on a large tract of land on Highway 316 near Fort McCoy. When on the job, he was a tough game warden who diligently protected our wild life.

First Sergeant Harold Rogers retired from the Florida National Guard and lives in Salt Springs. He was also a marine.

Don and Lois Winslow live on Highway 316. Don was in the Navy during WWII.

Herbert and Gracy Mann lived on Cemetery Road off Highway 19. When the Lord took Herbert to heaven, Charles, one of their sons, moved to Salt Springs to take care of Gracie. Charles served three tours in Vietnam as a Huey helicopter specialist. He is super-qualified on computers.

Reverend Miller, pastor of the First Christian Church in Salt Springs, performed the marriage ceremony for Phil Greenwell and his wife Linda. Phil, you will recall, was my company commander in Vietnam. The ceremony took place on our dock, and I walked Linda down the dock to Phil.

"Reggie" of Reis Pump Service on Highway 314 keeps us all supplied with wells and pumps for water. He can drill it, repair it, or sell you a new one – always with a smile!

Judy Collier of Salt Springs has been our representative to the Sheriff's Department of Marion County for many years. Again, service with a smile! Hal and Lisa Glenn are great people; Hal has his own business on Highway 319 supplying building materials, sand, rock, gravel and cypress mulch.

Paul and Juanita Meunier live on Lake George, seven miles south on Highway 19. Paul was on the Aircraft Carrier *Hornet* in 1942 when it took Colonel Jimmy Doolittle close enough to Japan to launch an attack with 16 B-25 bombers. Their air assault took place only five months after Pearl Harbor was bombed by the Japanese, the event that triggered the United States' involvement in WWII. Doolittle's daring raid raised the morale of our entire nation when we had been at war for only five months.

"Beep" and Carol Blanchard live at Eureka and are independent souls who can do almost anything – except during hunting season when you have to just leave Beep alone to let him hunt. Beep and Carol were always there when Peggy and I were in the hospital for her surgery. Always friends!

Bill Johnson and his wife Dale "The Realtor" are retired. Bill spent many years with Clay Electric and now operates the fitness center on Highway 314 in Salt Springs.

Jack and Dena Roig moved to Salt Springs last year from Plant City, and are great people and good neighbors. They just completed their second year with the Strawberry Festival as concessionaires, and they make absolutely the best Cuban sandwiches.

Roger and Linda Allhands are dear friends who live in Salt Springs. John and Jane Houch live on the north side of Lake Kerr. John loves sailing, and Jane is an artist, a very talented lady.

Bob and Jennie Blanton, who also live on the north side of Lake Kerr, are great people! Bob knows the most about the history of this area of anyone we know. He also makes knives and cases.

Master Sergeant Norman Melin and his wife Susan live on the south side of Lake Kerr. He is retired from the Florida National Guard and now works with the Guard in St. Augustine, driving back and forth to St. Augustine each day, a sign of great dedication!

Skip McDonald and his wife are weekend neighbors to the west. He is a lawyer in Ocala and his wife is a business lady. Their son is attending college and their daughter Allison is best friends with our granddaughter Martha.

June Bickmeyer, who had a large blueberry farm in Citra, was our neighbor to the east. Jim and Yvonne Dykes lived just two doors to the east. Jim gave Peggy a hard time about the Florida State University "Seminoles," since he was a University of Florida "Gator." We miss them.

Joseph and Engrid Lopes and their son David live in the vacation house on our right side. He runs the Coors distributorship in Ocala. Barbara Cato, one of our nearby neighbors and a true "Gator" fan, worked at Clay Electric for 25 years. She says I look like her father.

Nevin Durst rented our cabin for years and is a very happy person. He had two daughters who live out west. Mr. and Mrs. Miller, a couple from Michigan, also rented our cabin for about five months of the year. He is the brother of the pastor of the Christian Church on Highway 316. Gene Skillin rents our cabin all year now. He's retired from the Sarasota, Florida fire department and loves to hunt and fish.

There are several people in Salt Springs for special mention. Charlene and Dickie Johnson are our next door neighbors and close friends. They have a son, Rickie, 31 years old, and a daughter, Jody, 35 years old. Jody and her husband Jeff have a one-year-old son. Charlene was always there with smiles, jokes, and thoughtfulness. She would rather fish than eat. Dickie and Rickie, heavy equipment operators, have their own company. They always say, "Yes, ma'am" and "No, sir," which makes us feel 100 years old (we're *almost* there).

That "Gator" Hospital

While in Salt Springs, Peggy developed a pancreas problem. During 2005, Dr. Ashwin Rumalla of Ocala identified a "mass" in her pancreas. The mass was believed to be cancerous. He set up further study by Dr. Hemming, a surgeon at Shands Hospital, a part of the University of Florida Medical Center. Peggy elected to undergo surgery at Shands. On 14 November 2006, Dr. Hemming performed the "whipple" surgery. The mass, lymph nodes and portions of the stomach were surgically removed. The mass they removed from the pancreas was identified as a "neuroendocrine" type of cancer. The removal of the cancer was completely successful. Neither radiation nor chemotherapy was necessary.

After three and a half weeks in the "Gator" hospital at Shands, Peggy was sent to rehab at the Ocala Healthcare Center. She was in rehab three weeks longer while clostridium difficile ("C-Diff") was being treated. After several weeks at home in Salt Springs, she gained her strength back. I knew she was getting better when she began to complain about being sent to that "Gator" hospital!

C hapter 32
The New Generation

During the time that Peggy and I were living in Plant City and I was working with the festival, and later on when we started our new adventure in Salt Springs, so much happened with our sons, Kent and Scott. It would take many pages to detail all that happened, so only a brief recap of these events is included here.

Scott

Scott knew what he wanted, even in childhood. He wanted to be involved with nature, because he loved animals, fish and wildlife. To achieve that goal, he attended the Abraham Baldwin Agricultural School in Tifton, Georgia, where he was trained in wildlife management. He completed their degree program and worked for a time at a quail ranch in Georgia.

He then enrolled in the Florida Law Enforcement Academy in Tallahassee. Immediately after graduation from the Academy, he became an officer with the Fish and Wildlife Commission working for the State of Florida, where he is still employed.

He now has four horses and nine cows on a 36-acre ranch in Blountstown, where he built a beautiful house, and he loves living there. Being a game warden is his chosen profession.

Kent

Kent graduated from Florida Southern College in Lakeland, where he was very active in the ROTC program. He earned his paratrooper wings and Ranger tab at the ROTC summer camp. Upon graduation from college, he became a regular Army officer and chose armor as a service branch.

He served five years in the Army, both as an armor and an infantry officer. Peggy, Scott and I visited him in Bad Tölz, Germany.

After military service, Kent knew he wanted to sail. He participated in the Whitbred-Around-the-World race, which started in England. The crew of 15 sailors manned a 160-foot racing boat. He terminated his participation in the race and disembarked when they reached Cape Town, South Africa. He then continued alone on a journey to New Zealand, later coming back to South Africa, then going on to Zimbabwe.

Kent returned home and became the captain of the *Golden Hind*, a 17th Century English ship. It was on display in several U.S. ports. There he met the public relations lady for the ship, Caroline Smith. Kent and Caroline later married in England. Scott, Peggy and I went to their wedding in Linton, which is in North Yorkshire. Caroline's mother and father hosted the wedding. Mr. Maurice Smith and his wife Joan were most hospitable.

Kent and Caroline continued on to the University of Manchester in northern England, where Kent graduated with a master's degree in environmental biology. His degree was so impressive that the University of Kent offered him a Ph.D. (professor) in his chosen field. So, Kent and Caroline moved to nearby Whitstable, England, to study at the university.

While there, on 25 January 1996, Martha Christine Cassels was born. Peggy and I traveled to England to see our new grandbaby.

Kent and Caroline's marriage ended in divorce, but he enjoyed visiting rights with Martha for several years. He bought a boat in England and earned qualification as a sea captain, then became the skipper on several different sailing vessels. He spent a total of 20 years in England as a sea captain, coming back to America in 2009.

His profession has taken him back to sea, and he's now employed full time as the first officer on a 156-foot yacht. As I am writing this, he's either in the Virgin Islands, the Bahamas, or his home port of West Palm Beach, Florida.

Martha Christine

Martha, sometimes accompanied by Caroline, has visited us in the United States every year as she's been growing up. As I'm writing this, she's 16 years old. We hope that later in the year, she will vacation with us either at Salt Springs or in West Palm Beach. Kent will probably be here, too.

C'est la Vie

As it so often happens when the children you have loved and nurtured during their childhood and youth become adults, their schooling, interests and careers can take them in separate directions and far away. When you finally are able to stop and enjoy a free period in your lives, they are in the middle of the busiest times of their own lives and working hard in their chosen paths.

It was that way for us. Peggy and I had both our two boys together with us one Christmas day for the first time in 20 years.

Each one occasionally comes to stay with us at Salt Springs, and it is an understatement to say that we enjoy having them here.

C hapter 33
What Was It Like 40 Years Ago?
Bandido Charlie Explains

Obviously, no one person could have seen everything that was happening all around him, especially when he was engaged in a full-scale battle for his life against what was, as we determined later, an overwhelming force of enemy soldiers who were well equipped with ordinance that they were using against us with deadly efficiency.

The noise was deafening and the surroundings surreal – instead of what would have been, on a normal, peaceful day, a beautiful canopy of trees in a forest of green – there were the sounds of explosions and bullets, and the sight of men being hurt and killed. This was anything but a normal day.

Unless you have experienced something similar, it would be difficult, perhaps even impossible, to visualize or imagine the scene. Even in hindsight and more than 40 years after it took place, it is still amazing to me that my undermanned band of men was able to face down such a ferocious enemy force, and how they prevented, against truly overwhelming odds, being utterly annihilated.

To understand the complete story of those days in the fall of 1969, you have to hear it from other men who were there and who survived to tell it.

"C" Company of the 1/16th, also called Charlie Company and more famously known as Bandido Charlie, was led by Captain Phillip Greenwell. His first sergeant was Alfredo G. Herrera, and his track driver was Ron Mackedanz. All three men were involved in the events of the fall of 1969, and particularly those of 12 August 1969. In the years since returning from Vietnam, they all have told their stories of those events in print.

Phillip Greenwell's account of our engagements with the enemy in the fall of 1969 and his other experiences were memorialized on August 2, 2008, when he was interviewed by Steven Brown on behalf of Ball State University and gave his oral history, which is contained in V 269-13 of the university's Cantigny First Division Oral Histories. The video and text of his oral history are available, for now, on their website.

Alfredo G. Herrera, First Sergeant of Charlie Company, has written a book titled REACHING AN LOC, which includes his experiences in Vietnam. He is a member and officer of the current veteran's group of Bandido Charlies, and his book can be obtained directly from the Bandido Charlie Association website as well at various other sites on the internet. The Association's website address is www.bandidocharlie.com

Ron Mackedanz, hereafter often referred to as "Mack," was Phil's command track driver. Mack has been active in many local and national veteran's activities since returning from Vietnam, and is also a member of the Bandido Charlie Association. His biography and some other activities have been published on the internet, and there are excerpts of his Vietnam experiences posted on the Association's website in the history section. Ron's book, titled DRAFTED, has also been published.

With permission, excerpts of their stories are set forth below. Some paragraphs were broken into smaller segments for ease of reading, but the content is the same as originally published.

Captain Phillip Greenwell

The first major gunfight was on the 12th of August 1969. This was more or less a counterattack. We knew that the 9th NVA [North Vietnamese Army] Division had come into country and were operating and trying to attack the province capitals, and our goal was to interdict them and try to catch them trying to get back out.

We had pretty good intelligence because on August 10, a helicopter had spotted a large group of North Vietnamese soldiers. The Battalion Commander [Kenneth Cassels] took my 2nd Platoon and air assaulted in. I was not there, I had gone to Quan Loi. The Battalion was going to stand down there several days in the future; I was supposed to go there and find out where we would go, what the facilities were, what we could expect, what we needed and all that.

As we were going back, we started picking up radio transmissions, and that's how I found out that my platoon had been hauled off by the Battalion Commander. And he air assaulted them, captured some prisoners. The prisoners talked freely, and that's where he got the intelligence information of where we might be able to find some other guys fairly soon. Turned out it was correct, although we weren't quite as prepared for it as we thought.

In analyzing it today, I think I understand more about what had happened but it was a very sizable unit, probably 600 - 900 North Vietnamese soldiers. They were dug in … with heavy weapons, anti-tank weapons, RPGs (rocket-propelled grenades), recoilless rifles, heavy machine guns. I believe their goal was to make sure that when they attacked Quan Loi, reinforcements couldn't come down Highway 13 and couldn't take this back road to come in.

Alpha Company was in the lead, and they came to a bridge. We had an armored-vehicular launched bridge, which is a tank chassis with a bridge that scissors out. They had used this 'cause we knew we had a stream crossing to make. And apparently, they were having a little trouble getting across the bridge. Battalion Commander went forward to hurry things up – this is early in the morning, about 6:30 or 7 o'clock – then they got across the bridge. Well he [Cassels] stayed up in the front.

When we got to this T [in the road], the North Vietnamese opened up, 'cause it's a slight hill going up both ways – not a real valley now – but a very slight rise either way. On the other side of this road, the terrain dropped off pretty seriously. So they opened up and knocked out the first track – actually it wasn't the first track, we thought it was the first track at the time, turns out it was the second track of Alpha Company. Set it on fire.

Alpha Company in the meantime had run in here and they were bunched up, and they were fully engaged now from both sides and couldn't maneuver. I remember Col. Cassels just calling me, said, "Phil, get up here."

We were in rubber, but … right here to the north, there was a clear area in the rubber. Why, I don't know, it was clear – about the size of a football field or so. It was obvious Alpha Company was fully engaged and unable to maneuver, they were too close together.

Bandido Charlie's Initial Assault on 12 August 1969
Photo courtesy Phillip Greenwell

So I had a rifle company from the 1st Cavalry Division, Delta Co., 5/7th Cav. riding on my tracks with my company, so I asked them to dismount. We turned, dropped these guys off, and I maneuvered my folks up the hill and then turned, wheeled a little bit left – the idea being to come here, and take the pressure off of Alpha Co. so they could get out, and to give the North Vietnamese a real worry that they were going to be flanked. And it worked, and Alpha Company was able to get out. They pulled back.

Well, in the meantime the Battalion Commander's track had been hit, and his driver jerked the controls, track went back, hit a tree, knocked everybody off. Battalion Commander's maps went one way, he went another way, they had to get the driver evacuated, and then it got hit again I think. So, I couldn't call the Battalion Commander on the radio, there was nobody in – I got no answer at all. I could talk to battalion S-3, Maj. Jim Harris; he was in the air in a helicopter. He didn't know what had happened to the Colonel so I assumed the Colonel was dead. Turns out, he was just on the ground trying to find another radio and a ride to get back in the fight.

So we maneuvered up and took the pressure off, and Alpha Company – the bulk of their force, came behind us.... . And as we got to the top of the little rise there, that's when the North Vietnamese really opened up. They knocked four of our tracks out; mine was the first, almost instantly. It was kind of funny, they were shooting RPGs, and I remember one going right over my head. My driver thought it'd hit me, but it went right over my head.

Then we got hit once, then again. The first one blew the motor. The second one blew the inside out. 'Course it knocked us off the track.

Learned a valuable lesson that day. I carried a shotgun – I figured when it was time for me to start shooting, a shotgun was about right – but I had my web gear on the back of my seat instead of on my body. And of course, when I went off, the web gear was still up there with all my ammunition in it. So, I was going to get that, and a machine gun from the North Vietnamese stitched the seat and knocked all the shotgun shells everywhere. I looked like a squirrel trying to gather acorns, trying to pick shells up off the ground.

My First Sergeant, Al Herrera, had been on R&R. He'd just got back, and his track remained behind to guard the bridge that we had left to go across the stream. And I called him up, and said, "First Sergeant, why don't you get up here and ride with me? And tell me about R&R, I'm gonna go someday." So, he was sitting right here next to me. Well, he got hit, an RPG hit the track beside us and splashed out. He was trying to help some wounded soldiers, and it splashed out and got him pretty good. My driver, Ron Mackedanz, when the first one hit, it caved the side of the APC on his right side in, and crushed his arm a little bit.

He's sitting on the left front, down in the hatch. And he couldn't come back through the track, he was going to have to go out the top to the front where the enemy was. He had an M-79 grenade launcher, and he was using that with one hand, shooting at the enemy. The second RPG hit us, and it severely wounded our gunner, Al Kalchik, on the back on his legs, so the gun stopped. I was on the radio by that time trying to get air and artillery support and talking to Maj. Harris trying to find out why I couldn't talk to Col. Cassels, and trying to maneuver the Company.

Mack jumped out of the track, ran around behind, got Al down out of the gun hole. And got him back and they were working on him. Another RPG hit that wounded Al again – both Als, Al Kalchik and Al Herrera – medic came, Mack got up on the gun. Al had shot the riflings out of the barrel so he couldn't hit anything with it, but I handed him some ammunition anyhow. Another RPG hit and splashed Mack all down the side up here, and he dropped out of the hatch, screaming, "I'm hit! I'm hit!" I grabbed him, and I looked at him and said, "Mack, you're all right."

He said, "Oh." Was fine then. He wasn't all right, but he helped get the wounded down the hill. I told First Sergeant, said, "You get these guys down the hill." I didn't realize the First Sergeant was wounded as bad as he was, it didn't show exactly.

Actually what had happened, the second RPG that had hit had sent shrapnel up under Al's arm and cut this artery, and the medic couldn't stop the bleeding. And Al knew – course he's

First Sergeant – he'd been around this Army a long time, and this was his second tour. He knew things were going to get bad pretty quick losing this much blood, so he stuck his thumb in the hole, and had the medic tape his arm so his thumb wouldn't come out. Saved his own life. Stayed conscious and directed the evacuation of all these guys. Remarkable, remarkable.

Anyhow, they got down the hill and the other wounded got down. Forward Observer and I, finally he got down but I was down to one shot left and he was about out of ammunition. He got shot in the leg. I had gone forward and thrown a couple of grenades, 'cause I needed to see a little more of what was in front. And moved forward in front of the track – stupid, stupid amateur, stupid mistake.

Rubber plantations – every tree has its own water trap; it's just on one side of it. Well, there was this North Vietnamese soldier. He was just right in front of us, right behind this tree, and I walked right past him. And he stabbed me, just barely, I didn't even know he'd done it. I knew he'd come at me, and I shot him. I didn't know for two days that I had a cut here 'cause it didn't hurt. But he didn't shoot me, and I don't know why, but thank God he didn't.

But anyhow, I got back behind the tracks after that. That was a really stupid move. But I did see what I needed to see, and I knew that we were not going to be able to hold right here where we were, and we needed some air and artillery.

Was not allowed, I had talked to Major Harris on the radio, was not allowed to fire air artillery, gunships, nothing, no fire support.

They said that one of Alpha Co.'s tracks was missing, and we couldn't shoot for fear of harming our own soldiers. Well, as soon as I heard that, I got hold of my Weapons Platoon, my mortars, and instructed them to start knocking trees down. If nobody else was going to let me shoot their stuff I was going to shoot mine. 'Cause I could see, and there was no Alpha Co. track where I was going to shoot. But we couldn't knock the trees down, and we didn't have enough plastic explosives to blow it so that didn't work either.

Anyhow, FO got shot in the leg, I grabbed him, put him on my back and we went down the hill. Stupid soldier's humor. We kept falling down, was trying to go down a hill, you know, bullets are whizzing by, and he says, "You know, the only reason you're carrying me is cause that way I'm behind you and they'll shoot me first." And then we kept falling down and he says, "You're going to kill me! You just keep falling down!"

And then we got most of the way down, and it dawned on both of us at the same time, it was just like a revelation, because Alpha Co. had re-formed on the road, and the 5/7th Cav. soldiers were interspersed in between the Alpha Co. tracks. And he said, "You know Sir, if just one of those guys thinks we're VC they're going to chew us alive. Everybody's going to shoot at us." So we were just, "Oh please, don't mistake us for the bad guys." But turned out everything was okay, they didn't.

First Sergeant Alfredo G. Herrera

In June 1969 Cpt. Greenwell assumed command of Charlie Co., 1/16th Inf. (M). The vehicle crew Cpt. Greenwell inherited was composed of Spc. Ron Mackedanz, driver, Spc. Albion Kalchik, Track Commander (TC), Spc. Dennis Daughdrill, Pvt. Mike Renshaw, the RTO, the Artillery Forward Observer, 1st Lt. Knutsen, and the assistant Forward Observer, Spc. Siegel (the baby FO).

I was due for R&R so I left the company at the end of July to return to Lai Khe. Cpt. Greenwell told me to let him know about my trip and visit with my wife in Hawaii when I returned to the company. I told him that I would. We had no idea that it would be 30 years before we had a chance to discuss my trip to Hawaii.

I arrived back in the company area in Lai Khe on August 10, 1969. The company XO told me that the company had deployed north to the An Loc area. I could not leave alone as there was nothing traveling going in that direction to accompany me.

The next day, August 11, 1969, I noticed that the company had not taken the "water buffalo" (a water tank extremely essential for our tracks). I was very upset and told the XO that the company should not have left without the water. I found a track that was going north to the company area and had them hook up the water buffalo to their track. In the meantime, I sent the mail clerk, Pfc. Robert Dorris, to get the company Jeep.

Then in a convoy of two we set out for the company forward at An Loc. I did not know it at the time, but the company had been on 24-hour alert because elements of the 272nd and 273rd NVA Regiments were in the area.

We arrived to join the company without incident. I told Dorris to quickly return back to the rear in Lai Khe. I was worried about him but found out later that he had made it back safely. I joined my men and my 007 track. Most of us remained on alert and awake during the night.

In 2006, Herb McHenry and Ken Cassels supplied me with detailed information of an enemy encounter that occurred on August 10, 1969, just two days before August 12. Second Lt. George Perabo and members of his 2nd Platoon were assigned to search and destroy a reported NVA area. They boarded choppers for an Eagle Flight and traveled to the area, where they encountered and engaged in enemy fire.

Some of the platoon members participating were Herb McHenry, Don Lane, Gary Hummer, Pat Delaurie, John Hanrahan, Greg Goldenstein, Ralph Rome, Melvin McElreath, (Doc) Joe Gossett, and Platoon Sgt. Marion Culbertson. As the enemy fire began, the men of the 2nd Platoon returned fire, killing several enemy soldiers and capturing four prisoners. They brought the prisoners to the rear for interrogation, where the prisoners provided extremely valuable and accurate information covering projected enemy activities.

The operation in which we were participating was designated *Operation Kentucky Cougar.*

Very early in the morning of Tuesday, August 12, 1969, we joined the Battalion Commander, Lt. Col. Cassels, and assorted battalion staff, Alpha Co., 1/16th and elements of Delta Co., 5/7th Cav. for a combined search-and-destroy mission. We formed our tracks at the departure point and proceeded to begin the operation. We reached an area where there were soldiers from an engineer unit with an AVLB (Assault Vehicle Landing Bridge).

I can't recall whether it was emplaced, but Cpt. Greenwell told me to remain with my track and crew of Sgt. Richard Burkardt, Spc. Massey, and Spc. Hill, and secure the AVLB and the engineers. I thought this might be boring, so I had Burkardt radio to the command track and ask Cpt. Greenwell if I could come and ride on his track for the operation. Cpt. Greenwell assented, and I ran to his track at the head of the company column.

We were traveling on an access road following Alpha Co. when we heard that Alpha was taking fire from the rubber trees. We were heading west at the time and then turned north alongside Alpha Co. into the rubber trees heading towards the enemy fire. All of our .50-cal. machine guns were firing, and most of the men began firing their own weapons. We were approximately 50 yards into the trees when we began taking heavy RPG fire. I knew our men were firing their M-79 grenade launchers, and at first I thought some were firing very close to our tracks. Then I realized that it wasn't M-79 fire, they were RPG rounds dropping all around us.

I began feeding ammunition to the machine gunner, Spc. Kalchik, who was firing as fast as he could. I would give Kalchik cans of .50 cal. ammunition each time he emptied the previous can. I know we were hit once because I heard the round as it hit the front of the track. The driver, Spc. Ron Mackedanz, was hit with that round. I was in the process of handing Kalchik another can when the next round hit right in front of us, wounding us both. We tumbled from the track onto the ground.

Mackedanz and a few others reached us to help, as Kalchik and I were very badly wounded. I didn't realize how bad the wounds were. We were both hit in our upper body area. The medic came about then and tried to stop the bleeding from my wounds in my upper right arm area. He couldn't, and I told him to leave and treat the other wounded. He left, and I decided then that I was not going to bleed to death right there, and jammed my thumb into the wound. I finally got it to stop bleeding.

We couldn't have been on the ground for more than two or three minutes when another RPG round exploded between Kalchik, Mackedanz, and myself. The second round hit Kalchik and me. This one hit us in the lower extremities, somehow missing Mackedanz.

By then, other men arrived to help us and, since Kalchik couldn't run, four men got a litter and began carrying him to the rear. I don't remember all of them, but two of the four men carrying Kalchik were Spc. Melvin McElreath and Mackedanz.

As the four men were carrying Kalchik, McElreath was shot by AK-47 automatic rifle and hit in the stomach. He fell on Kalchik, but being a large man, McElreath regained his feet and the four men continued on to the dust-off helicopter. I can't recall all the men, but I know that Mackedanz and McElreath distinguished themselves on this day.

I ran to the track and opened the rear door. I saw Cpt. Greenwell holding his shotgun; he had been firing a 12 gauge. I thought he had run out of ammunition. Thirty years later, in August 1999, I met Phil Greenwell at a BRO reunion in Louisville, Kentucky. One of the first things I asked him was how come he had run out of ammunition so quickly on that date. He told me that he didn't run out; he had dropped all the rounds on the floor of the track and was trying to retrieve them.

We both thought it was humorous 30 years later, but on August 12, it was very serious.

Cpt. Greenwell maintained his composure, rallied the company, and repelled the enemy. On August 12, 1969, Cpt. Greenwell's leadership throughout the action was evident and had immense impact on the ultimate favorable results of the engagement. Cpt. Greenwell received a Silver Star for his actions on that day.

I left the CO and looked out across the field and saw all the men firing. I remember one sergeant, but cannot remember his name. He was in the second platoon and was just firing away. The reason I recall this image is because he was wearing a black beret. I had tried to make all the men wear their steel helmets, and it was very clear that he was not. I don't fault him and never will because he was exposing himself to enemy fire and returning it as fast as he could. I can still picture him. In fact, I was very proud of him on that day.

I also saw the Battalion CO, LTC Cassels. He was on the ground, but I couldn't tell what he was doing. At a later BRO reunion, he told me that an AK-47 hit and wounded his driver's arm. The driver could neither maneuver nor stop the vehicle, the track began to run erratically, causing LTC Cassels to fall to the ground. LTC Cassels also dropped his maps and was picking them up, which is what he was doing when I saw him. As Battalion Commander, he was the instrumental officer, calling in fire, etc., and the maps were extremely important.

The enemy drew us in perfectly; we could not fire flares nor smoke through the rubber tree canopies. We had no way of telling the artillery and air where we were located. It was obvious that the North Vietnamese were very well prepared for this engagement.

I began running to the rear. I couldn't hold my rifle, so I just had my .45-cal. pistol in my left hand. I doubt if I could have hit anything, but that was all the firepower I had. My right arm was completely useless. At the time I didn't know how much damage had been done to my lower extremities. As I was running to the rear, the enemy was firing their AK-47s at us. I could hear the rounds whistling all around me. I would stop behind a tree for a rest, and the rounds would hit the trees.

It was very scary because I could hear the rounds flying past my ears (it certainly wasn't like the movies). I felt very threatened and wasn't sure I could make it out on my own. I finally did and reached the area where the wounded were being loaded onto a track to be transported to the dust-off helicopter.

I was trying to get everyone loaded onto the track and had to order some of the men to get aboard. A few wanted to stay, but most were severely wounded and could not have been much use on the battlefield. Mackedanz recalls this very well, as he said I ordered him to "get on the damned track." I then got on myself. I was surprised to see my TC, Sgt. Burkardt, Hill and Massey. It was my #007 track that was transporting the wounded! They had come forward when they heard all the weapons firing. They loaded and carried us to the dust-off area where we were boarding the choppers.

I made a feeble attempt, as I was extremely weak, to direct the loading of the wounded. About that time Spc. McElreath got hold of me and lifted me into the chopper. I didn't, nor could I, resist. What made me feel worse at the time was that McElreath had been shot in the stomach. He was seriously wounded and still managed to lift me onto the chopper next to the door gunner. He was a very heroic man on that day, and I feel that he should be recognized for what he did carrying Kalchik and placing me on the chopper when he himself was severely wounded. For their actions, I feel that both Mackedanz and McElreath should have been awarded a valorous medal or citation.

Before I was placed on the chopper, I gave Burkardt my situation book (which has been very instrumental with dates and names of my time in Bandido Charlie), my pen and pencils, address book, my holster, pistol, and my strobe light. I asked him to send everything home to me. He said he would. However, I never received my pistol or strobe. But I really didn't think the military would allow him to mail these two items. I am grateful for him and for the items he did manage to send.

When the chopper lifted off, they made a circle around the ground area. I waved at my crew and they waved back. Hill even waved a "V for peace" sign.

What happened next was related to me by Sgt. Don Baum, also a patient while we were at Letterman Army Hospital at the Presidio of San Francisco. Sgt. Baum told me that Burkardt and crew were returning to pick up more wounded when the track came under heavy RPG fire. They returned fire, with Hill on the .50-cal. machine gun, Massey was driving, and Burkardt was in my place as NCOIC of the track. Hill was hit and knocked off the track. Massey jumped up to begin firing the .50 and was also shot off the track. At that time Burkardt got off the track, picked up each man and placed them on the track, got in, and drove the track away as RPG rounds were firing all around them.

Sgt. Burkardt received a Silver Star for his quick and heroic actions.

I didn't know of this action because at the time we were flying to the aid station. We circled the aid station area, and I saw many enemy bodies on the wire. The NVA had almost overrun the aid station. Fortunately, they were repelled, but many were still on the wire, dead.

When we landed, the medics rushed us in. Almost everyone but me was on a litter being treated. I was standing, leaning on a crate or something when I began to feel very weak. I called a medic over and he saw my legs covered in blood. He tore my trousers and saw my leg was messed up and had me lay down on a litter. I found out then how much damage had been done to my left leg. I was bleeding very badly from those wounds.

I was laying there, it could not have been more than 10 minutes, and looked up to see Hill and Massey being brought in to the aid station! I was very surprised and disappointed, because they were both hurt pretty bad. I looked at Hill and called his name. All he could manage to say was that they were ambushed. I did not have an opportunity to ask more of Hill, as the medics picked up my litter and I was taken to another helicopter and transported to the 121st Evaluation Hospital and home of the 25th Inf. Div. in Cu Chi.

Spc. Ron Mackedanz

Preface

Around the first week of August, Bandido Charlie saddled up and headed up Highway 13 toward An Loc and Loc Ninh. These two areas were receiving a lot of activity from the North Vietnamese Army (NVA) and the Vietcong (VC).

On 12 August 1969 Bandido Charlie, along with Alpha Company, and a Company from the 5/7th Cavalry, went to bring the Cavalrymen out toward the Cambodian Border. The convoy consisted of Charlie Company with 20 APC's, Alpha Company with 20, and Battalion Headquarters with about 6 APC's. There were also about 150 men on foot with them. They were moving through the rubber plantations west of An Loc.

As they were going through the plantation, a couple of NVA soldiers ran across the road in front of the column. The Battalion Commander (LTC Kenneth Cassels) ordered four tracks to pursue the enemy. The NVA led them straight into an ambush. They all turned to the right, heading toward the ambush to provide support for the four tracks.

Suddenly they started to take heavy fire from the left flank. They swung around and proceeded up a hill in the direction it was coming from.

They were up against the 272nd NVA Regiment with reinforcements from the 273rd NVA Regiment. They were dug in and ready for action. The U.S. soldiers were outnumbered two to one.

The Battle in Ron's Words

As we moved into the ambush site, Alpha Company on the left, LTC Cassels in the middle, and Bandido Charlie on the right, we charged ahead. The Cavalry troops had dropped off to cover our right flank and rear. The NVA were dug in, tied up in rubber trees, and firing at us from every possible position. With the Bandido Charlie command track leading the way, we let 'em have everything we had.

The NVA knew what they wanted to accomplish. Within the first half hour of the firefight, they took out the Battalion Commander's track and both company command tracks. I guess they knew how to count radio antennas.

Driving for Capt. Greenwell, I saw the first RPG go right over my head. We were within 20 to 30 yards of where the NVA were dug in. I didn't see the next RPG. It hit the front of our track, destroying the engine. The service door in the driver's compartment blew out and hit me in the shoulder.

Bandido Charlie Co. Command Track July 1969
l-r: Ron Mackedanz, unknown, Al Kalchik,
Capt. Phil Greenwell, Dennis Daughdrill, Spc. Siegel
Photo courtesy of Ron Mackedanz

At that point, I must have developed tunnel vision, because all I remember seeing was little brown guys all over in front of me. I grabbed my M-79 thump gun (grenade launcher) and started firing from the driver's hatch.

I didn't realize at the time that there was no one left on my track. They had all been blown off when the RPG hit.

After what seemed like forever, I crawled out of the top of the driver's hatch. Al Kalchik, my fifty gunner, told me just a couple of years ago that he ran up and told me to get the hell out of there.

When I got to the rear of our track, Al Kalchik and 1st Sgt. Al Herrera were both there. I didn't realize that they were both already wounded from the initial RPG hit. As we hunkered down for a minute, another round came in from somewhere. Although we were all very close to each other, I was not hit, but Kalchik and Herrera were both hit seriously. I was hollering for a medic while I was cutting Kalchik's pant leg off and bandaging up his wounds as best I could. 1st Sgt. Herrera was hit in the main artery near his armpit. He had shoved his thumb in the wound to stop the bleeding.

Finally a medic got there and took over. Not knowing what to do next, but realizing that we had nobody on our 50, I went through the back hatch, into the track, and up on the 50. Believe me, this was no hero thing. It was survival.

Inside the track, Captain Greenwell was trying to coordinate the support. At that point he believed that Lt. Colonel Cassels was out of the fight. After getting on the 50, I started firing at the NVA positions. Unfortunately the barrel on the 50 was burned out and rounds were going all over the place. Tracer rounds were going in six-foot circles.

I got off about 100 rounds or so and Capt. Greenwell was handing me more ammo, when another RPG with my name on it hit in the trees just behind me on my right side. I took multiple shrapnel hits in my right hand, right shoulder, back, face, and the most serious ones in the neck. The biggest one just missed my jugular by about a quarter of an inch.

I remember dropping down inside the track saying, "I'm hit, I'm hit." Capt. Greenwell took one look at me and said, "You're all right Mack, get out of here."

Years later he told me, "You looked pretty tough Mack, I didn't think you were going to make it." I was covered pretty heavy with blood, some mine, some Kalchik's.

When I baled out of the track, the medic was still there working on Kalchik and 1st Sgt. Herrera. He bandaged my neck and hand wounds and told me to get the litter out of the track so we could get Kalchik out of there. I got the litter and we loaded Kalchik on it. Then with 1st. Sgt. Herrera running alongside barking out orders, Mel McEldridge, I and two other guys grabbed the litter and started running down the hill with Kalchik on it.

We hadn't made it very far when McEldridge took a round through his side that exited by his navel. He fell, and I stumbled and fell on him and Kalchik. We got up, grabbed the litter again, and took off for the medevac track at the bottom of the hill.

Update

In the end, Ron and the others were medevac'd out. Ron was choppered to the 12th Evacuation hospital at Cu Chi where they removed most of the shrapnel from him. He spent a few days there and then was sent to a convalescent hospital in Cam Rahn Bay for a few weeks.

Around the second week of September, he returned to Lai Khe and Bandido Charlie. He had less than a month left in Vietnam.

Ron has little recollection of his remaining time in Vietnam. A new first sergeant tried to make Ron go out into the field, but Capt. Greenwell stood up and said "No!" Ron never had to go back out.

Ron went up for promotion and was promoted to the rank of Sergeant just before his tour of duty ended in Vietnam. He left Vietnam 11 October 1969 and arrived back in the U.S. on 13 October. When he awoke on the morning of the 14th, there were three inches of snow on the ground, a big change from the jungles of Vietnam.

Kenneth G. Cassels

The details of the foregoing stories by three of the Bandidos were related to me through interviews with them during the eight reunions of the Big Red One I have attended, beginning with the first one which I attended as a guest of the Bandido Charlie Association in Reno, Nevada in August 2003.

The individuals are identified in their stories: Captain Phil Greenwell, 1st Sergeant Al Herrera, and Spc. Ron Mackedanz.

Captain Greenwell of Charlie Company, Captain Olson of Alfa Company, and the commander of Delta Company, 5/7th Cavalry, were company commanders on 12 August 1969 in Vietnam, *"the day which will live in infamy."*

I was the battalion commander who led all three companies against an enemy that had been identified by North Vietnamese prisoners of war captured by an assault team from Charlie Company on 10 August 1969. Al Herrera and Ron Mackedanz related their accounts of these events to me at the reunion in 2003.

The enemy contact was made about 7:15 a.m. on the morning of 12 August 1969. I was riding in the fourth track back from the lead element of Alfa Company when it took the first RPG hit. After the NVA attack began, I directed Phil Greenwell to move his company forward to line up on the right side of Capt. Olson's Alfa Company and give them support. Phil reacted immediately, and their stories tell the rest.

It had been my job as the battalion commander to guide the combined arms force to find and close with the enemy. My last order given was to ask Phil Greenwell to commit his Charlie Company on the right side of Alfa Company, because I had been thrown to the ground immediately after my driver's right arm had been hit by an enemy AK-47 round. Yes, I was the one that Al Herrera saw crawling on the ground "lower than a snake's belly."

In an infantry company, the primary responsibility of the unit rests with the company commander. Since I was temporarily out of action, it was up to the individual company commanders to influence the fate of their units as best they could. On 12 August 1969, that responsibility fell to Capt. Olson, Capt. Greenwell, and the commander of the elements of Delta Company, 5/7th Cavalry.

This was during a critical period when all the previous training of a unit had to come into play. That training obviously was very effective, as everyone involved in the battle – whether officer or enlisted, lieutenant or private – had to assume a leadership role as individual circumstances demanded it from them. These well-trained soldiers rose to the occasion.

Throughout the nine hours of that day-long battle, it was attack and counterattack, give a little, take a little. We were fighting on an area no larger than a football field all day, but with my radio out of commission I knew only what I could see just in front of me.

With the three companies, we had a total of about 40 APCs firing at the same time, with each track firing their organic weapons, including the .50-cal. guns, and each soldier firing his personal arms.

During the first 45 minutes after the initial contact with the enemy, several of our soldiers were evacuated by chopper to medical facilities where they could get treatment for their injuries. Those who were still able continued the fight for another eight hours.

Mission Accomplished

The battle on 12 August 1969 is referred to as an ambush by some. I don't take exception to this term, but I think it could be referred to as a deliberate, planned attack. The intelligence gained by interrogation of the four prisoners of war captured on 10 August 1969 told us where to find the NVA units. Our mission for the next 48 hours would be to close with and destroy or capture the enemy.

Search and destroy missions are a normal part of combat. Because of the intelligence we gained on 10 August, we didn't have to search very far before we found the enemy we were looking for. It was obvious at first contact that the enemy had no intention of being captured or surrendering, making our course of action quite clear. Regardless of the terms used, the 40 APCs and their well-trained crews won the battle on 12 August 1969. I was privileged to be a part of the nine-hour combat operation.

As the Bandidos related to me their own personal stories of how it was for them 40 years ago, much of which I was hearing for the first time, I felt again the tremendous pride that I had felt then for all the units involved and the resourcefulness of the individual track leaders and their reactions to the situation.

The courageous and valiant response by individuals on that day accounted for the outcome. We won the battle. We closed with the enemy, destroying enough of them so that by the end of the day, the enemy didn't want any more of what our "gutsy" forces had to offer. The men of Alfa, Charlie, and Delta Companies lived up to the mission of the infantry: *close with the enemy and destroy or capture him*. The enemy was good, but our forces were superior. I express my heartfelt thanks to these men.

C hapter 34
Honorary Colonel of the Regiment

Now back to Salt Springs and retirement.

As Peggy and I were enjoying retirement, we were asked by Col. "Skip" Baker, the 2011 Honorary Colonel of the Regiment (HCOR, 16th Infantry Regiment, 1st Infantry Division (the Big Red One)), to attend his investiture of Distinguished Members of the Regiment (DMORs) at Fort Riley, Kansas. We traveled to Fort Riley, and at the investiture he announced that I had been approved to take his place as the new Honorary Colonel of the Regiment.

Ken with his wife, Peggy Sparkman Cassels

Skip's health had been failing. You see, Skip participated in the liberation of Kuwait in 1991. Saddam Hussein set the oil fields in Kuwait on fire, and Skip had breathed in that awful smoke. Over time, it had adversely affected his lungs. Even at his last investiture ceremony, he was forced to stop, catch his breath, and use oxygen to finish. Skip then excused himself, and he and his wife Kathryn went to their car and drove to their home in Texas.

Skip asked that Peggy and I, along with Al Herrera, Honorary Sergeant Major of the Regiment (HSMR), and his wife Betty, stay and pay our respects to LTC Kevin Lambert, the battalion commander of the 2/16 Infantry Battalion. This request included Col. Lambert's command sergeant major.

We agreed to stay, and Col. Lambert asked all of us to attend the battalion's banquet and dinner. Al Herrera, as Honorary Sergeant Major of the Regiment, would help with the presentation of awards and I would be introduced to the ladies and gentlemen as the new HCOR. Al had been in place for three years prior to this event with Skip Baker.

Col. Lambert asked me to address those gathered for the occasion. Shannon, Kevin's wife, asked that I address the wives in particular, as the battalion soldiers were preparing for combat deployment early the next year. Peggy and I know how it is to be separated from your loved one for a year or more. Army wives must be a special breed, as they put up with so much from their husband's chosen career. It is now an all-volunteer military force that we are dealing with. Shannon said I did okay, and that the wives appreciated my comments.

Skip conducted two investitures and left three for me to do at the next BRO reunion at Buffalo, New York in August 2011.

The HCOR / DMOR / HMOR Program

October 10, 2011 was chosen as a target date for the distribution of guidance to all current DMORs and HMORs. This guidance would include the criteria to be used by the nominators and the nominees in the selection process for the most deserving DMORs/HMORs for 2012. This is the update sent out, and it includes the guidance criteria:

Update on Activities of
the DMOR Program
May 15, 2012

This is my first activity update to the DMORs/HMORs since becoming HCOR. I expect to provide periodic updates on the program to you and to the Regimental Association during the upcoming year.

Often, the HCOR is asked: "How and when did you become a DMOR?" Well, I first learned of it when I opened my mail one day in early December 1986, and there was a plaque signed by the Commanding General of the 1st Infantry Division. The certificate was dated the December 1, 1986. What a surprise! It indicated that the DMOR was in recognition of achievements perpetuating the lineage, honor and traditions of the regiment. Indeed, it was an honor to be a Distinguished Member of the 16th Infantry Regiment, and I knew immediately that Maj. Gen. Albert Smith was the one who nominated me.

Maj. Gen. Smith was a combat veteran of World War II. As a lieutenant, General Smith fought in North Africa, Sicily, and Italy. His unit was brought back to England and on 6 June 1944, he went ashore at Omaha Beach as part of the 1st Battalion, 1st Infantry Division. I served the General as a Battalion Commander when he was Assistant Division Commander of the Big Red One in Vietnam. It was a pleasure to see his helicopter land at the battalion command post on a frequent basis between April and June of 1969. Years later, Gen. Smith became the first HCOR of the regiment.

Many years later, Col. "Skip" Baker asked me to take his place as the Honorary Colonel of the Regiment (HCOR), due to his health. He had been the HCOR for seven years. "Skip" was observed conducting an investiture that made several candidates DMORs. During June 2011, I filled in for him at Buffalo, New York, at the 2011 BRO reunion when several more, who were unable to be invested at Fort Riley, became DMORs or Honorary Members of the Regiment.

On 10 October 2011, as the new HCOR, my guidance on how to become a DMOR was published and distributed to all DMORs. It included specific information for the nominator as well as the nominee and was quite detailed. My guidance letter of 10 October 2011 was sent to all DMORs with attachments and the e-mail, U.S. Postal service, and the telephone were used to try to get all DMORs/HMORs informed as to how the program under the new HCOR would operate.

It wasn't long before it was known that many did not get the guidance. Some DMOR addresses had been changed; some didn't have e-mail capacity; some DMORs didn't respond. Obviously, the DMOR roster we were using was not up to date. So, in October 2011, a major effort began to update the roster. That effort has been ongoing ever since last October.

Sgt. Maj. Herrera has been working on the update of the DMOR roster, and the revised roster has been forwarded to the First Infantry Regiment Association's webmaster for publication.

In late December 2011, as the HCOR, I was truly pleased that eleven nominees and one HMOR would be recommended to become a DMOR or HMOR. These recommendations were forwarded to the appropriate authority in accordance with Army Regulation 600-82. All eleven nominees were approved. These approved certificates have been framed in preparation for an investiture to be conducted by the HCOR in 2012 during Victory Week for the 1st Infantry Division at Fort Riley, Kansas.

The investiture was set for 12 June 2012 at 10:00 A.M. at the 1st/16th Infantry Commander's headquarters, Lt. Col. Roger Crombie was to be host for the investiture. Col. Crombie and his staff worked out the details and Sgt. Maj. Alfredo Herrera, U.S. Army (retired) undertook responsibility for the dissemination of information pertaining to the investiture and Victory Week to be conducted 11-14 June 2012.

Since 9/11 the BRO has been at war for a period spanning more than ten and a half years. During this time, elements of the regiment have been deployed to the Middle East in Iraq and Afghanistan at least three to five times. I'm proud that the eleven approved inductees included several active Army officers and NCOs. Other inductees served in Vietnam and the Middle East. All had very impressive records of service in the regiment.

The regiment consists of two infantry battalions, the 1st of the 16th and the 2nd of the 16th. The 1st Battalion members call themselves "Iron Rangers," and the 2nd Battalion call themselves "Rangers." All are part of the BRO, the "Big Red One."

During the month of March 2012, Sgt. Maj. Herrera and I traveled to Fort Riley with our wives, Betty and Peggy, to accomplish several things for the regiment and the DMOR program.

In late December, Lt. Col. James Smith, Commander of the 1st Battalion, BRO, had just returned to Fort Riley from Afghanistan with all of his combat-seasoned men. This was an accomplishment worthy of emulation.

Lt. Col. James Smith celebrated the battalion's return to Fort Riley with a banquet in honor of all of his brave soldiers and their wives. The Colonel invited the HCOR and Sergeant Major to sit at the head table. Peggy and Betty were seated near Col. Smith's wife Debbie and the brigade commander. Such an honor.

The banquet was so impressive. After the dinner, which was so well prepared, each of the Colonel's subordinate commanders came forward and told Col. Smith that their unit was so proud and appreciative of his leadership, particularly during combat. Further, that their unit would be proud to serve him in the future.

The second accomplishment is attributable to Lt. Col. James Smith. We witnessed an awards ceremony which he set up and orchestrated. The company commander of those receiving the awards [Captain Phillip Greenwell] worked three and a half years putting together the documentation required by the Department of the Army for approval of four silver star awards and two bronze star awards. The citations were for combat actions that took place on 12 August 1969, some 43 years ago, near An Loc, Vietnam.

All awards were for heroic actions against the 272nd and 273rd units of the 9th North Vietnamese (NVA) Division. The action on that day took place in a rubber plantation beginning at dawn on 12 August 1969 and continuing for a long nine hours. The heroic award recipients were outnumbered on that day at least three to one by the NVA. The NVA division was good, but the friendly task force was supreme, partly because forty .50-cal. machine guns from two mechanized companies had been brought to bear at dawn. By late afternoon, the 9th Division forces slipped back to safer haven in Cambodia.

On 12 August 1969, the NVA force wounded Al Herrera several times, and he lost a lot of blood from one of those hits to a major artery. Al's recovery took place stateside and took many months in the hospital. For his actions in that engagement, Sgt. Maj. Herrera has been awarded the Silver Star on two occasions, first by the Governor of Oregon and the second at Fort Riley. The Governor of Oregon appointed Al to the Advisory Council of the Oregon Department of Veterans Affairs. As HCOR, I am proud to have this senior NCO as an able assistant.

Another accomplishment for the regiment was the change of command ceremony for Lt. Col. James Smith and Lt. Col. Roger Crombie, a spectacular and moving event which we were privileged to attend. Prior to the ceremony, Al Herrera and I enjoyed conversations with Lt. Col. Kevin Lambert, 2nd Battalion Commander. He was there to pay his respects to Jimmy Smith and Roger Crombie. Col. Lambert had been training hard for some time, preparing for his battalion's deployment and commitment to combat. [As of this writing, the 2/16th Battalion has now been in Afghanistan for about eleven months.]

When the change of command ceremony was over, we rushed to return to the Kansas City airport to turn in our rental car and go to our respective departure airlines.

The visit to Fort Riley over a period of about five days was in a congenial atmosphere that we enjoyed everywhere we went, and we had the opportunity to exchange ideas pertaining to improving the DMOR/HMOR program in compliance with Army regulations.

The Regimental Association president, Robert Humphries, was well represented by Phil Hall and his wife. At Fort Riley, we met many soldiers who were in perfect physical shape, as well as some who were Wounded Warriors. The wives and families of the soldiers seemed to be happy and proud to be a part of the armed forces—they are Army strong!

Peggy and I, along with Al and Betty, looked forward to going to Fort Riley for Victory Week June 11-14, 2012.

I take pride in representing DMORs everywhere. Thanks for allowing me to provide a thumbnail sketch of how the DMOR program is being implemented.

Respectfully,

Ken Cassels
Honorary Colonel of the Regiment

Well, that was the beginning of my three-year tour as the HCOR. The response was heartwarming and investitures were, for the most part, conducted at Fort Riley, Kansas in June 2012. LTC Roger Crombie, the new battalion commander of the 1st/16th Infantry Battalion, 1st Infantry Division, participated.

Col. Crombie and his command sergeant major attended the 2012 reunion of the 1st Infantry Division August 1-5, 2012 in Memphis, Tennessee. Peggy and I, in my official capacity as the HCOR, also attended this reunion. It was during the reunion that we learned of the passing of Skip Baker, and it was there that we observed a moment of silent prayer in honor and memory of his service to our country. May Skip rest in peace.

The end of the 2012 reunion ended the duties of the HCOR for 2012. Two more years as the HCOR, 2013 and 2014, will complete my three-year assignment and commitment to administering the DMOR/HMOR program. Completion of the 2014 year will also mark our return to enjoying retirement.

In the meantime, any monies realized after expenses of publication of this autobiography will be donated to the Gulf Ridge Council of the Boy Scouts of America.

Thank you and may God bless. ~ Ken Cassels

Col. Kenneth G. Cassels
U.S. Army (Retired)
Honorary Colonel of the Regiment 2012-2014
16th Infantry Regiment, 1st Infantry Division

C hapter 35
A Small Town Heritage

My life began at birth on 24 December 1926 on West Tever Street in Plant City, Florida. Thus, a subtitle for this book could have been "*A Small Town Heritage.*" I am proud to claim Plant City as my heritage. At least for the first thirteen to fourteen years as I grew up, my values were formed in that small town. Memorizing the Boy Scout law, the oath, and the motto, I attempted to adhere to the values set forth by the Boy Scouts of America as principles and guidance for my life.

Reynolds Street
a main thoroughfare in Plant City (circa 1925)
a year before the author was born
from the Burgert Bros. photographic collection (late 1800s-1960s)
Courtesy Tampa-Hillsborough County Public Library System

My heritage includes being a member of a loving family: my father, mother, and two sisters. All played a major role in my development, and now all have gone to be with the Lord. May the good Lord bless and keep them in the palm of his hand. Though some of the family are mentioned from time to time in the book, no attempt has been made to name all of them, as this is an *autobiography*; the book is about a guy named Ken.

20 November 1955, as described in this book, changed a way of life. Peggy Sparkman and I were married in that small town of Plant City. From that day forward, the two of us would become husband, wife, parents and grandparents, sharing all that was to come thereafter. As I write this, Kent and Scott are in their early fifties and Kent's daughter, Martha Christine Cassels, who lives in England with her mother, is 16 years old and off to college.

Peggy and I are thankful that the Lord has blessed us with a great family. I will be 87 in December, and Peggy will be 83 in August. We both are relatively healthy and both of us have enjoyed a life that is expected to continue. We thank God for being American, and fervently say, *"May the Lord bless the United States of America."*

L-R: Peggy Sparkman Cassels, wife of Kenneth G. Cassels
Scott G. Cassels, son of Ken and Peggy
"Dog" and Martha Christine Cassels (Kent's daughter)
Kent Lamar Cassels, son of Ken & Peggy, and
Kenneth G. Cassels

C hapter 36
A Matter of Honor

It is not the end of my journey — but this book is finished. Now to get it published! If successful, proceeds less the cost of printing and publication will be donated to the Boy Scouts of America, Gulf Ridge Council, at 13228 North Central Avenue, Tampa, Florida.

The writing of this book is all about growing up during my early years in Plant City, a very small Florida town. My core values have roots there. These values are attributed in part to the following:

> Dr. Wilbur Hicks, Scoutmaster
> Eagle Scouts Wilbur Hicks, Buddy Blain,
> C. B. Nuckols, Mac Smith, and others

Being an Eagle Scout was truly an honor.

In conclusion, the Scout Law, the Scout Oath, and the Scout Motto of *"Be Prepared"* all influenced me and my small-town heritage and values. I have never forgotten the twelve points of the Scout Law, that a Scout should be *Trustworthy, Loyal, Helpful, Friendly, Courteous, Kind, Obedient, Cheerful, Thrifty, Brave, Clean, and Reverent.*

On my honor, I did my best to do my duty to God and my country, and to obey the scout law; to help other people at all times; to keep myself physically strong, mentally awake, and morally straight.

Kenneth George Cassels
The End — for now!

Epilogue

I have been in contact with many of the individuals whose names I mentioned in this book and have previously related a little of their current status. You may find it interesting where life has taken some of the others, so I have set forth just a few of their stories, in no particular order. Before those updates, however, I'd like to relate one event that particularly struck a chord with my own family.

Gail Wilson

My wife Peggy and a friend traveled to Washington, D.C., to look at The Wall. She was looking for one name in particular: Gail Wilson. As Peggy and her friend were searching The Wall, they were unaware of the other people around them, so focused were they on the name they were attempting to find. Suddenly Peggy saw the name and spoke it aloud: *Gail Wilson.*

Immediately, a young man standing near them asked, *"What did you say?"* Peggy turned around and repeated the name, *Gail Wilson.*

The young man paused for a moment, then said quietly, *"He was my father."*

Peggy and her friend were astonished. Then the young man told them that he had come to visit the Wall for the first time in his life. His mother had been so devastated by his father's being killed in action in Vietnam that she had always refused to talk about him, so he knew nothing about his father except that he had died in Vietnam. His mother had always refused to let him come to see the Wall, but he had decided to come now that he was old enough and on his own. He wondered if Peggy and her friend would be willing to tell him what they knew about the father he had never had a chance to know. Their hearts were saddened and touched by the young man's story, and they related to him everything they could remember about his father, Gail Wilson.

Mickey Purchet

Mickey Purchet (*per-shay'*), a platoon leader in Charlie Company who earned the Silver Star for his bravery in action on 5 September 1969, continued his military service in the Florida National Guard, rising to the rank of full Colonel ('06).

Jeff Frayne

Jeff Frayne retired from his business, and it is now closed. Someone told me she used to shop in the Lakeland store where his designs were sold, and she was surprised one day to find it had been closed. She says it is a shame, too, because the clothes were exactly the style she liked to wear, were of very good quality and were offered at a good price.

Jefferson Thomas Frayne passed away during 2011, and I was honored to participate in the eulogy for my classmate. We graduated from Gulf High School in New Port Richey in 1944.

Roy Parke

News stories have said that Roy Parke owned a red Cadillac and had a swimming pool shaped like a strawberry. It is fact that his produce stand, Parkesdale Farm Market, is one of the busiest tourist attractions in Plant City; tour buses still jam the parking lot during the strawberry harvest. His strawberry shortcakes and shakes are deemed the best in the county, maybe all of Florida. Sadly, Roy has passed on, but the market is still there and still the best.

A Tribute to Mary Jones

This book would never have been written if it had not been for the professionalism of Mary Jones, who typed my manuscript. She gave me encouragement through the hard part, that part dealing with the great responsibility of leading brave

Americans against the 9th NVA Division elements in Vietnam. She graduated from Plant City High School here in Florida. It was easy for us to relate to each other, since the Florida Strawberry Festival was known to each of us. I thank her from the bottom of my heart and have the deepest respect for her.

Medals Awarded After 43 Years

In 2011, the Department of the Army announced its approval for the award of medals to the following members of Bandido Charlie, 1st Battalion (Mech), 16th Infantry Regiment, 1st Infantry Division, for valorous actions in the Republic of Vietnam on 12 August 1969.

The official presentation of these awards by the Commanding General of the First Infantry Division was held on March 9, 2012, at Fort Riley, Kansas after the Iron Rangers returned from their deployment with the Joint Special Operations Command, Afghanistan.

These long-overdue awards were made possible by the invaluable support received from Major General (Ret) Albert E. Milloy, Jr., Colonel (Ret) Kenneth G. Cassels, and Kentucky Congressman Ben Chandler.

Phil Greenwell, who was Company Commander of these men on 12 August 1969, took three and one-half years of his life preparing the documentation to support these awards. Forty-three years late, the presentations were witnessed by Phil and myself on March 9, 2012 at Fort Riley Kansas.

The Silver Star
<u>for Gallantry in Action</u>

Alfredo G. Herrera, Beaverton, Oregon, presented by the Governor of Oregon and Division C.O. at Fort Riley

Ronald W. Mackedanz, Kandiyohi, Minnesota, at Fort Riley

Douglas J. Ludlow, Battle Creek, Michigan, at Fort Riley

The Bronze Star
<u>for Valorous Achievement</u>

Stephan J. Biernacki, Jr., Ashley, Pennsylvania, at Fort Riley

Roger Haynie, Benton, Arkansas, presented by the Governor of the State of Arkansas in the Governor's offices, since Roger Haynie's health prevented him from traveling to Fort Riley

Silver Star Medal
*Third highest medal for valorous
actions against the enemy*
Second highest is the
Distinguished Service Cross (DSC)

Bronze Star Medal

Appendix A
Timeline

December 24, 1926	Born in Plant City, Florida to Samuel G. Cassels and Alma Watson Cassels
1929	Stock market crash, Great Depression
February 1930	First Strawberry Festival in Plant City, coronation of Charlotte Rosenberg as first Strawberry Queen
1931	First grade at Woodrow Wilson Elementary School, Plant City
1934 or 1935	New house in Plant City with all the comforts of electricity and indoor plumbing
1934 – 1938	Sister Marguerite completed high school in Plant City, went to Florida Southern College, began teaching career, met and married Fred K. Marchman in New Port Richey
1937	Move to Miami, first paying jobs, beginning of interest in aviation
1938	Boy Scouts
1939	Moved to Wildwood, earned rank of Eagle Scout, played saxophone in high school band
1939	Sister Christine completed high school in Plant City, obtained business degree at Tampa school, began work as a teletype operator and office manager in Tallahassee, married Robert (Bob) C. Zimmerman.
December 7, 1941	Pearl Harbor attacked; U.S. entered WWII
March 31, 1942	Father died at Marguerite's home in New Port Richey. Returned to Wildwood and lived with grandmother Ollie Watson.
1942 – 1944	Moved to Marguerite's home in New Port Richey. Worked as volunteer fireman, soda jerk, truck driver, grocery store clerk, driving Model A Ford. Also had a job pumping gas, changing oil and filters. Graduated from Gulf High School in New Port Richey in 1944.

July 28, 1944	At 17, sworn in to the Army Air Corps as an Enlisted Reserve (ACER) at MacDill Army Airfield in Tampa.
1944 – 1945	Trained at Clemson College, a military engineering school in South Carolina. After schooling 1944-1945, formally inducted into Army Air Corps and sent for basic training to Keesler Army Airfield at Biloxi.
	Gained leadership skills on the job by being assigned to take charge of Flight No. 1 through basic training course. Learned to shoot, move and communicate.
1945	Transferred to Scott Army Airfield in Illinois to train as a cryptographer. Received security clearance and received orders for the Pacific-Far East Command.
August 1945	Japan officially surrendered, ending WWII.
December 1945 to December 1946	Shipped out to serve in Occupational Forces in Japan, as orders still stood even after WWII ended in late 1945. Arrived in Yokohama at 18 years old, continued on to Irumagawa and finally Showa to work as a cryptographer for one year, assigned to 7th Air Service Group, 5th Air Force in Showa.
	Celebrated 19th birthday at Showa.
December 15, 1946	Shipped stateside; discharged from the Army with rank of corporal.
1947	Civilian occupations included Tarpon Springs fisherman and working for a construction contractor in new Port Richey.
1947 – June 1951	Entered University of Florida, joining Kappa Alpha fraternity and ROTC, received training at Ft. Benning. Korean War began while in training at Fort Benning in 1950.
	Commissioned to rank of Second Lieutenant of Infantry in June 1951.

August 1951	Graduated University of Florida with BSE (Education) and began teaching school at Bradford County High School. Received offered for regular Army commission
September 25, 1951	Committed to 4 years active duty as regular Army commissioned officer upon completion of one-year teaching contract.
1952	Completed contract to teach school at Bradford County High School.
June 1952	Began military service, sent to Ft. Benning for more training, then taught new recruits at Fort Jackson, SC. Learned of upcoming assignment for active combat duty in Korea.
1953	Met my future wife, Peggy Sparkman, in Bradenton, Florida.
1953	Shipped out to Hokkaido to retrain First Cavalry Division in preparation for commitment to combat duty in Korea.
	Assigned as a platoon leader in Love Co., then transferred to be the new company commander of King Co. and winter training.
March 25, 1953	Promotion to First Lieutenant. Summer training near Chitose.
1954	Korean War ended with a signed truce. First Cavalry Division moved south near Tokyo to continue training. Assigned as S-1 (Adjutant) of the battalion.
	End of 4-year commitment to regular Army.
September 25, 1954	Decided to make the Army a career and continue assignments.
1955	Returned stateside for reassignment as ROTC instructor in Waterbury, Connecticut.
November 20, 1955	Married Peggy Sparkman in Plant City, Florida. On return to Waterbury, Connecticut, Peggy experienced first airplane travel and sight of snow.

1957	Transfer to Fort Benning.
August 21, 1957	Birth of first child, Kent Lamar.
1957	Pathfinder school, provided navigational assistance to Army aircraft through selection of landing areas and drop zones. Put Paratrooper tab on uniform.
1958	Army Ranger training at Dahlonega, Georgia, and Yellow River, Eglin AFB Florida. Put Ranger tab on uniform. Now 32 years old.
October 25, 1958	Promoted to Captain, transferred to Ranger Department at Fort Benning to teach offensive and defensive tactics.
	Was "lane grader" for West Point cadets.
January 26, 1960	Birth of son Scott George on 26 January 1960 in Tripler Army Hospital at Fort Benning.
1960 – 1961	Reassigned for one year of language training at Monterey, California. Earthquakes and Pacific runs. Began learning Arabic from instructors from Baghdad, Iraq. Assigned quarters at Fort Ord.
1961	Short assignment in Washington, D.C., attending ten-day course at the State Department for diplomacy training prior to mission in Saudi Arabia to teach their airborne battalion military tactics.
1961 – 1962	Began one-year assignment in Saudi Arabia by traveling through Portugal, Madrid, Libya and finally to Dhahran and Jidda, Saudi Arabia. Met Lt. Col. Ruzzi of the Royal Saudi Arabian Airborne Battalion. Learned to scuba dive with the sharks and some of the personnel of the U.S. Air Force.
	Toured the Holy Land and met and talked with the King of Jordan while in Jerusalem.

August 1962 - 1964	Reassigned to the G-3 (Operations) Section of the 82nd Airborne Division at Fort Bragg, North Carolina, dealing with highly classified material. Went to Homestead AFB during the Cuban missile crisis as a coordinator and representative of the division and the 18th Airborne Corps.
January 22, 1963	Promoted to temporary rank of Major, reassigned to C&GSC.
1964 – 1965	Command and General Staff College (C&GSC) at Fort Leavenworth, KS.
September 27, 1965	Promotion to permanent rank of Major.
1965 – 1968	Reassigned for three-year tour to CINCPAC at Camp Smith, a Marine base at Oahu, Hawaii just above Pearl Harbor. Lack of available base housing required purchase of a house in Kailua.
November 4, 1966	Promoted to Lieutenant Colonel 4 November 1966, assigned to Intelligence Section of CINCPAC. Job required travel all over the Pacific to places like Saigon, Vietnam, Thailand, Japan and Singapore.
1967	Moved to Fort Shafter, lived there for a year as war in Vietnam escalated.
September 1968	Arrived at Tan Son Nhut Air Base at Saigon, assigned to the First Infantry Division – the "Big Red One." Processed at "Di An" before going to Lai Khe, division HQ, then to the 1st Brigade operational base at Quan Loi.
	Duties included monitoring night radio transmissions from deployed units and the tactical radio net; investigating casualties caused by choppers inserting patrols in prohibited areas; daily inspections of perimeter defenses; responding to attacks as directed by the brigade commander.
	Also assigned as coordinator for a new operation to open a road between Phuoc Vinh

	and Song Be, remained at Phuoc Vinh for extended period before returning to Lai Khe. Met Charlie Rogers who later was awarded the Medal of Honor.
October 21, 1968	APC's of 5/60 Infantry (Mech) transferred to 1st Infantry Division (the "Big Red One") as new 1st Infantry Battalion, under command of Lt. Col. Shuffstall until April 1969.
	At Phuoc Vinh, Rome plows begin to cut a wider road to reopen Highways QL-14 and 311 from Dong Xoai to Song Be.
April 8, 1969	Assumed command from Col. Shuffstall of the 1st Infantry Battalion, 1/16th Infantry Regiment (Mech), 1st Infantry Division.
	Continued Rome Plow Operation providing security detachments for several U.S. and ARVN engineer companies.
	Constructed several fire support bases and sent out ambush patrols. Became familiar with APCs and directed modifications to tracks by removal of steel plating.
June 15, 1969	First convoy rolled unmolested along the entire route from Saigon to Song Be, ending the VC's domination of Phuoc Long Province
June 1969	FSB Jim established. Hawaii R&R
July 25, 1969	Maj. Gen. Orwin C. Talbott gives 60-minute notice to move the battalion to the vicinity of An Loc and meet Col. Leach of 11th ACR.
	Established temporary and permanent NDPs and fire support bases: 1/16, HQ and Charlie Co. at FSBs Allons II, Alfa Co. at FSB Eagle II about 8 kilometers north of An Loc.
July 30, 1969	President Nixon visits the BRO.
August 1969	Operation Kentucky Cougar and the Battle of Binh Long Province commence.

August 10, 1969	Bandido Charlie conducts air assault near An Loc, captured four NVA and learned of the 272nd and 273rd NVA Regiments' plans to capture An Loc.
August 12, 1969	Col. Leach directs an attack against the NVA regiments, which are pursued and engaged. The ensuing 9-hour battle was waged against the enemy by Iron Rangers elements that included Olson's Alfa Company, Greenwell's Charlie Company (the "Bandidos"), and 7th Cavalry troops.
August 13, 1969	Attempted to determine effectiveness of 12 August battle. (I never believed in "body count"; we looked for indications of how effective we were on 12 Aug. 1969.
September 5, 1969	Responded to ambush by 273rd NVA against 1st Platoon of Alfa Company, Alfa and Charlie Companies mount an attack. Close call from "friendly fire" averted by Sergeant Stephen Rabourn. Shrapnel injuries received from RPG near-miss.
September 20, 1969	Termination of Operation Kentucky Cougar. Iron Rangers return to base to be welcomed by new division commander, Maj. Gen. Milloy, division staff, and the BRO band standing at the gate.
September 22, 1969	General Milloy conducts change of command ceremony of 1st Battalion 16th Infantry (Mech) to LTC David C. Martin.
September 23, 1969	Vietnamese awards and decorations, a couple of Silver Stars, Legion of Merit, two Bronze Stars, 11 Air Medals, and a new assignment to the Pentagon. choppered out through Saigon for journey home.
October 1969–1972	Four years at Pentagon-intelligence specialist.
July 12, 1972	Promotion to rank of full Colonel.

July 1, 1973 – March 31, 1975	Served 1-1/2 years in Atlanta as Infantry Readiness Coordinator, US Army Readiness Region IV, Ft. Gillem, Forest Park, Georgia.
April 1, 1975 – June 30, 1978	Assigned as Chief, US Army Readiness Group Patrick at Patrick Air Force Base, Florida. Mission was to influence National Guard and Army Reserve units throughout the State of Florida.
May 22, 1978	Received the State of Florida Governor's award, the "Florida Distinguished Service Medal," for outstanding meritorious service.
June 30, 1978	Retired from the Army.
December 1978 – July 1, 1981	Taught special needs classes at Dover school, established "DoverCraft Industries" and program model to meet the special requirements of the students, including a woodworking shop. where students produced products for sale.
September 1, 1981	Began employment as General Manager of the Strawberry Festival in Plant City, Florida, a second civil career that lasted 14 years. Understudied E. O. "Davvy" Davenport until first "solo" festival February-March 1982.
April 30, 1982	Took full charge of Strawberry Festival as manager after retirement of Davvy Davenport on April 30, 1982.
April 30, 1995	Retired from managing the festival
January 30, 1998	Moved to new home Salt Springs
2003	Attended first Bandido Charlie and Big Red One reunion in Reno in August 2003.
June 2011	Announced as Honorary Colonel of the Regiment for 2012-2014

Appendix B
Military Education

Infantry School	Infantry Unit Officers' Course	1952
Fort Benning, GA	Advanced Course #1 31 weeks	1958
	Airborne Course #11 3-1/2 weeks	1958
	Ranger Course #11 7-1/2 weeks	1958
	Pathfinder Course 6 weeks	1958
	Instructor Training Course #2 4 weeks	1958
US Army Language School Monterey, CA	Arabic Language Course 47 weeks	1960-1961
Military Assistance Institute Washington, DC	Diplomacy (focus on Saudi Arabia) 4 weeks at State Department	1961
C&GSC Ft. Leavenworth, KS	Officer's Course 38 weeks	1965
Infantry School Fort Benning, GA	Special Vietnam Orientation Course 1 week	1968
Big Red One Vietnam	Leadership Course Under Actual Combat Conditions	1968-1969
Army General Staff Ft. Meade, MD	National Cryptology School 3 weeks	1970
Intelligence School Ft. Holabird, MD	Industrial Security Course 1 week	1970

Glossary and Abbreviations

ARR IV	Army Readiness Region
ACER	Army Air Corps Enlisted Reserve
achios	snow sleds
ACR	armored cavalry regiment
Alfa or Alpha	phonetic designation of a company-size force, *e.g.*, Company A
AO	area of operations
APC	armored personnel carrier
Aramco	Arabian American Oil Company
Arty	artillery
ARVN	Army of the Republic of Vietnam (South Vietnam)
AVLB	Assault Vehicle Landing Bridge
Bandido Charlie	Company C, 1/16th Inf. (Mech), 1st Division
Brig. Gen.	Brigadier General
BRO	1st Infantry Division, U.S. Army - the "Big Red One"
C ration	individual canned, pre-cooked, and prepared wet ration designed for use by soldiers on combat assignment
C&GSC	Command & General Staff College
cal.	caliber
Capt.	Captain
C'est la vie	That's life!
CINCPAC	Commander-in-Chief Pacific
C Company	1/16th Inf. (Mech), 1st Infantry Division, a/k/a Bandido Charlie
chopper	helicopter
CO	Commanding Officer

Col.	Colonel
CP	command post
CTZ	Corps Tactical Zone
Device	In military context, refers to an insignia added to a medal to further indicate the importance or meaning of the medal (*e.g.,* "V" for valor)
DSC	Distinguished Service Cross, second highest award for valor
DMOR	Distinguished Member of the Regiment
FO	forward observer on a track, from artillery
FSB	fire support base
G-1	Adjutant of the Division
G-3	Operations Section
Gen.	General (rank)
GPS	global positioning system
GS	General Service, referring to a pay grade for civilian employees
HCOR	Honorary Colonel of the Regiment
HQ	headquarters
HSMR	Honorary Sergeant Major of the Regiment
hull defilade	"Hull" refers to the tank's bottom section; "defilade" is to shield or conceal, hide by the use of natural or artificial obstacles; so "hull defilade" indicates that the tank's main body has been positioned to obtain concealment and protection against enemy fire
influence	in the context of actual combat, cause a desirable action to happen
influencing	imparting knowledge of procedures, skills and training to enable combat readiness; cause to happen
Iron Rangers	1/16th Infantry (Mech), 1st Infantry Division

KIA	killed in action
KP	kitchen police (cook, serve, clean)
lowboy	large open-bed trailer
Lt. / LTC	Lieutenant / Lieutenant Colonel
LZ	landing zone
Maj./ Maj. Gen.	Major / Major General
Mech	mechanized
MGs	machine guns
MOH	Medal of Honor, the highest medal awarded for valor
MIA	missing in action
NCO	non-commissioned officer
NDP	night defensive position
NVA	North Vietnamese Army
organic weapon	Weapons that are assigned to the unit, over which the unit leader has direct control.
POW	prisoner of war
PTSD	post-traumatic stress disorder
R&R	rest and recuperation
Refuse the flank	A military tactic utilizing a specific formation to (1) defend itself by preventing an attempted flanking assault by the enemy or (2) entice the enemy to attack its seemingly exposed flank, then assaulting the enemy with its main force.
	The defense maneuver: the unit's flank (side) about to be attacked regroups and forms an oblique angle* to its main body and turns to face the enemy in defense of its position. (*45 degrees or more). [As an *attack* posture, the maneuver is the same, but the main body then directs its forces in an assault on the enemy.]

Revetment	In military engineering they are sloped structures, formed to secure an area from artillery, bombing, or stored explosives. Barbed wire fences formed barricades against these forces.
RIF	reconnaissance in force
ROTC	Reserve Officer Training Corps
RPG	rocket-propelled grenade
RTO	Radio Telephone Operator
rubber	rubber trees of the Terre Rouge plantation
S-1	Battalion Adjutant
S-2	Battalion Intelligence Officer
Semper Paratus	Always Ready
TC	track commander
TF	Task Force
The Wall	Vietnam Veterans War Memorial
thump gun	grenade launcher
track	Armored Personnel Carrier (APC)
VA	Veterans Administration
VC	Viet Cong
WIA	wounded in action
WPA	Works Progress Administration
XO	Executive Officer

Index

References to major places, individuals and events that played a recurring role in the life of the author may appear only at the first mention in a chapter. Page ranges are given for some events. Some titles have been used so interchangeably that they may be referred to differently and appear on multiple pages; *e.g.,* the 1/16th Infantry aka Iron Rangers; Company C or Bandido Charlie; etc.

1

1/16th Inf (Mech), 1st Inf Div (Iron Rangers), 60, 61, 69, 70, 74–84, 86, 144
10 August 1969, 176, 178
11th Armored Cavalry Regiment, 70
12 August 1969, 80, 81, 84, 144, 145, 158, 159, 166, 167, 169, 172, 176, 177, 178
121st Evaluation Hospital, 172
13 August 1969, 80
143rd Transportation Brigade, 100, 106
15 December 1946, 22
150 azaleas, 147
18th Airborne Corps, 69
1st Brigade, BRO, 54, 55, 59, 60
1st Cavalry Div., 28, 30, 31, 74, 75, 86, 161, 196, 223
1st Cavalry Div., 3rd Brigade, 72
1st Cavalry Div., Delta Co., 5/7th Cav., 161, 167, 176, 177, 178
1st Infantry Division reunions ('03-'09), 145

2

2,000 wooden toys, 146
20 November 1955, 188
214th Regional Forces Co., 82

272nd NVA Regiment, 74, 75, 78, 145, 166, 172
273rd NVA Regiment, 74, 75, 81, 93, 166, 172
2nd Lieutenant of Infantry, 25

5

5 September 1969, 81–84, 93, 191
5/60 Infantry (Mech), 60
5th Air Force, 21
5th Battalion, 7th Cavalry, 76

6

6 August 1945 Hiroshima, 18
6 June 1944 *Operation Overlord*, 15

8

8 May 1945 (VE Day), 17
82nd Airborne Div., 46, 47, 48, 86

9

9 August 1945 Nagasaki, 18
9th ARVN Regiment, 4th Battalion, 75
9th NVA Division, 72, 74, 84, 93, 159

A

ACER (Enlisted Reserve), 15
achios, 30, 203
Aircraft Carrier *Hornet*, 152
Al ham Dulilla!, 54
Alfa Company, 65, 69, 70, 72,
    77, 79, 81, 93, 146, 160, 161,
    162, 164, 165, 167, 172, 173,
    176
Allhands, Roger and Linda, 153
Allons II, 82
Alpha Co. (see also Alfa Co.), 69
aluminum foil sugar bowl, 36
American Legion building, 124
Americus, Georgia, 41
AmVets, 151
An Loc, 56, 70, 72, 74, 75, 84,
    145, 166, 172
Anderson, Albert Jackson
    (Cactus Jack), 150
Anderson, Charles, 94
Anderson, Charles & Pat, 89
Anderson, Pat, 94
antique curiosity, 2
APC wooden replica, 144
APCs, 60, 61, 63, 172
April 30, 1995, 137
Arabian American Oil Co., 46
Arabic language, 42–46
Army Air Corps, 11, 15, 17, 129
army brats, 48
Army General Staff, 202
Army National Guard, 95
Army paratrooper, 38
Army Promotion Board, 105
Army Ranger, 39, 103
Army Regulation 380-5, 91
Army Reserve, 95, 98, 99, 100,
    103, 201
Arnold, Phil, 146
ARR IV, 95

ARVN (Army of the Republic of
    Vietnam), 63
Askew, Michael T., 146
Assistant Chief of Staff for
    Intelligence, 90
Atlanta, 95–97
Atlanta Army Depot, 95
atomic, 18
August 10, 1969, 74, 145
August 11, 1969, 76, 166
August 12, 1969, 76–81
August 2001, 142
Aulusio, Quincy, 146
azaleas, 147

B

B-24 bomber, 44
Baker, Kathryn, 180
Baker, Shannon, 180
Baker, Sidney F. "Skip" (Col.),
    179
Balcom, Imogene, 13
Ball State University, 159
Banana River, 98
Bandido Charlie Assoc., 145,
    159
Bandido Charlie Co., 63, 69, 74,
    81, 142, 192
Bandido Charlie Reunion, 142
Bandido Charlie's story, 158
Bandido Charlies, 144
barbed-wire fence, 4
barefoot in the sand, 4
Barnes, Bill, 148
Bass Champions, 148
Battle of the Bulge, 16
Baum, Sgt. Don, 171
Berry, A.L. (Al), 134
Bickmeyer, June, 153
bicycle paper route, 13
Biernacki, Stephan J., 146, 193

Big Red One, 54, 56, 60, 81, 85–87

Big Red One band, 86

Big Red One reunion, 176

Biloxi, 16

Binh Long Province, 72

Blain family, 7

Blain, Lester, Jr., 8, 24, 34, 189

Blanchard, "Beep", 140, 152

Blanchard, Carol, 152

Blanton, Bob and Jennie, 153

blue crab, 147

blue flame, 35

blue-eyed Russian, 93

boxing gloves, 7

Boy Scout camp, 7

Boy Scout Troop 4, 5, 136

Boy Scout Troop 5, 5

Boy Scout Troop 882, 94

Boy Scouts Court of Honor, 8

Boy Scouts Court of Review, 8

Boy Scouts of America, 5, 186, 187, 189

Bradenton, 27

Bradford County High, 25

Bravo Company, 71, 72

Brigade Duties, 58

Bright's disease, 12

BRO, 71, 74, 81, 144

BRO reunion, 142, 168, 169

Brocato, LTC Walter A., 99

Brocato, Peggy, 99

Bronze Star Awards, 193

Broogeman family, 7

Brooks, Bobby, 123

Brooks, Patsy, 117, 131

Brooks, Scott, 123

Brown, Steven, 159

Buck & Bass, 149

Buffalo, New York, 35

Bullard, Maj. Gen. K. C., 101, 102, 105

bulldozer (Rome Plow), 62

bullets and strawberries, 137

Bung, Gen. Nguyen Thoi, 72

Burkardt, Sgt. Richard, 167, 170, 171

Burkhalter, David and Diane, 149, 150

Burlington, Vermont, 116

Bush, Pres. George W., 143

buttoned up, 61

C

C rations, 66

Cactus Jack, 150

Calhoun, Joe, 146

Cam Rahn Bay, 175

Cambodia, 56, 72, 78

Camp Smith, 49, 50

Camphee Banks (Mexico), 23

candlelight, 2

Cangelosi, Karen, 149

Cantigny First Division Oral Histories, 159

Captain (rank), 39

Carlton, Bruce and Patsy, 52

Cassels' Account, 176–77

Cassels, Alma *Watson*, 1, 2, 34, 37, 40, 43, 94

Cassels, Christine, 1, 11, 34

Cassels, Kent Lamar, 37, 41, 43, 46, 49, 50, 52, 69, 88, 94, 96, 97, 103, 106, 155

Cassels, Marguerite, 1, 11, 12, 20, 23, 34

Cassels, Martha Christine, 151, 153, 156, 157, 188

Cassels, Samuel Gamble, 1, 4, 5, 8, 10, 12

Cassels, Scott George, 40, 41, 43, 46, 49, 50, 52, 69, 88, 94, 96, 97, 103

Cato, Barbara, 153
Chandler, Ben, 192
Channel 13 WTVT, 133
chaperone duty, 36
Chapman, Patricia, 34
Charlie Company, 65, 172
Charlie Company's story, 158
Charlotte, Vermont, 116
Chennault, Gen. Claire Lee, 11
Chicago, Illinois 2004, 145
Chitose, 31
christening water, 46
Christian Church, 154
CINCPAC, 49, 54, 88, 203
Citra, 153
civilian educator, 114
Clark family, 4
Clark, Bud, 125, 130
Clark, M.P. (Bud), 134
Clearwater, 14
Clemson College, 15, 16, 17
Cocoa, Florida, 98
Coffey, LTC Vernon C., 72
Collier, Judy, 152
Colonel (rank), 94
Colorado Springs 2008, 145
Columbia River, 20
Columbus, Georgia, 37
Command and General Staff
    College, 48, 49, 54, 95
Company C, 1/16th Infantry –
    Bandido Charlie, 63, 69, 142
Conner, Lily Zo, 13
Contingency Plans Area, 47
Corbin, David, 118, 120, 124,
    127, 128, 131
Costich, Capt. Kenneth J., 63,
    146
Costoff, Maj. Pete, 49
Costoff, Midge, 49
Coto, Tina, 52
Council for Exceptional

Children, 114
Country Music Assn, 126
Court of Honor, 8
Court of Review, 8
Creek, 45
Crombie, Roger (LTC), 185
Crow, Fred and Mary, 49
cryptographer, 20
Cu Chi, 172
Cuban missile crisis 1962, 69
Culbertson, Sgt. Marion, 166
Curtis Publishing Company, 5
Custer, George, 150
cyclone alarms, 49

D

D Co., 5th Battalion, 7th
    Cavalry, 76, 77, 78
D-8 bulldozer, 62, 66
Dahlonega, 39, 40
Danger forward, 85
Daughdrill, Spc. Dennis, 165
Davenport, E. O. "Davvy, 114,
    117, 121
Davies, 1st Lt. Billy T., 34
Dearborn 2009, 145
December 24, 1926, 1
Decubelis, Johnny, 13
DeKalb County area, 96
Delaurie, Pat, 166
delivering groceries, 13
Department of the Army, 26
Desert Storm 1991, 135
Detroit, 35
Devour 6 radio call sign, 82
Dhahran, 44
Di An, 54
Dickens, Susie Gardener, 135
Dingman, Lois, 13
discharge from Army, 22
DiSerafino, 2nd Lt., 31

Distinguished Military Grad, 26
Doolittle, Colonel Jimmy, 152
Dorris, Pfc. Robert, 166
Dover, 43, 50, 109
Dover Industrial Arts, 111
DoverCraft Industries, 112
Down Home, 146
Draft, Jackelyn, 13
DuBose, Darlene and Wally, 149
Durst, Nevin, 153
Dykes, Jim and Yvonne, 153

E

Eady, Carolyn, 117, 120, 124, 125, 127, 131
Eagle Scout, 8, 84, 189
earthquake zone, 41
Eglin Air Force Base, 39
Elfers, 13
Emerson, Lt. Col., 48
Enlisted Reserve (ACER), 15
Enola Gay, 18
Ergle family, 7
Ergle, Mrs. Clifford, 12
Essex Junction Fair, 116
Everidge, Cecil and mom, 134

F

Fairfax, 89, 94
Festival Carriage House, 127
Festival Expansion, 127
Festival General, 137
Figuero, 2nd Lt. Ruben O., 31
final exam question, 36
Finnell, John, 146
fire engine jockey, 13
First Lieutenant (rank), 31
Fish Hook, 54, 56
fishing on the Ocklawaha, 147
fit like a glove, 139
Fitch, Billy, 127

fletchettes, 57
Flight 1, 17
flight home to America, 87
Flight No. 1, 16
Florida Distinguished Service Medal, 105
Florida National Guard, 97
Flying Tigers, 11
Ford Falcon station wagon, 41
Fort Benning, 25, 26, 27, 37, 38, 39, 70
Fort Bragg, 46, 47, 48
Fort Gates Ferry, 151
Fort Gillem, 96
Fort Holabird, MD, 202
Fort Jackson, 27
Fort Leavenworth, 48, 202
Fort McPherson, 96
Fort Meade, MD, 202
Fort Ord, 41, 42, 43
Fort Riley, Kansas, 179
Fort Shafter, 51
Fowler, Sebert, 148
Frayne, Mary, 129
Frayne, Thomas Jefferson (Jeff), 13, 14, 21, 129, 191
Frayne's Sportswear Mfg., 129
Freeman, Capt. Ernest L., 71, 72, 144
FSB Allons II, 70, 74, 83
FSB Eagle II, 70
FSB Jim, 69, 70, 74
Fuell family, 4
Future Farmers of America, 115

G

G-3 (Operations) Section, 47
Gator Hospital, 154
Gault, Dawin ("Buddy"), 146
Georgia, 25, 26, 37, 38, 39, 70, 95, 96, 100, 103, 132, 150,

155
Georgia Slim, 150
Germany, 92
Gibbs, Louise, 117
Glenn, Hal and Lisa, 152
Goldberg, Sherwood, 146
golden bird, 88
Goldenstein, Greg, 166
Good, Bob, 146
Gossett, Joe ("Doc"), 166
Grandmother Ollie, 10, 12
Great Depression, 3, 15
Greenville, SC, 16
Greenwell, Capt. Phillip, 69, 74,
    77, 79, 82, 94, 144, 146, 152,
    158, 159, 165, 167, 168, 169,
    173, 174, 175, 176, 177, 192
Greenwell, Linda, 152
Greenwell's Account, 159–65
Griggs, Wallace, 149
Gulf High School, 13, 21, 23, 24,
    129
Gulf of Mexico, 23
Gulf Ridge Council, 186, 189

H

Hair Solutions, 149
Hanoi, 56, 72
Hanrahan, John, 166
Harrel family, 7
Harris, James, 1st Lt. & Doris, 48
Harris, Major James (Jim), 69,
    80, 86, 93, 101, 144, 162
Harrison, Joe, 151
Hart, Lloyd, 134
Hayes, Cora, 151
Haynie, Roger, 146, 193
HCOR, 179, 185
HCOR 2011-Skip Baker, 179
Headquarters-Army Readiness
    Region (ARR IV), 95

Hemming, Dr., 154
heritage, 187, 188, 189
Herndon, Azalee, 13
Herndon, Jerald, 13
Herrera, 1st Sgt. Alfredo G., 144,
    158, 159, 162, 163, 174, 175,
    176, 177, 192
Herrera, Al and Betty, 180
Herrera, Gene, 146
Herrera's Account, 165–72
Hessians, 76
Hicks, Dr. Wilbur Sr.,
    Scoutmaster, 7, 43, 189
Hicks, Wilbur, 7, 21, 24, 27, 34,
    189
Highway 13, 54, 72, 74, 75, 86,
    160, 172
Hill, Spc., 167, 170, 171, 172
Hillsborough County Fair, 114
Hiroshima, 18
Histories (see Cantigny), 159
Hokkaido, Japan, 28
Holt, Winfield, 2nd Lt., 31
Holy Land, 46
homecoming, 88, 89
Homestead Air Force Base, 48
Honeymoon Island, 14, 21
honorary Bandidos, 143
Hood, Rufus, 146
Houch, John and Jane, 153
Howsare, Valerie & Mike, 149
HSMR, Honorary Sgt. Maj. of
    the Regiment, 180
hull defilade, 28
Hummer, Gary, 166
Huron family, 4

I

I Am An American Soldier, 220
IAFE, 117
ice plant, 1

icebox, 1
II Field Force, 61
III CTZ, 63
Iliwahi Loop, 50
Illinois, 20
Industrial Arts, 111
Infantry Coordinator, 95
Intelligence School, 202
Intelligence Section, 51
interviews, 144
Iron Rangers, 192
Iron Rangers (see 1/16th), 60–94
Irumagawa, Japan, 20
Israel, 46

J

Jahn, Chester, 146
January 30, 1998, 140
Jebel Dhahran, 46
Jenkins, Clayton, 128
Jerusalem, 46
Jester, Niles, 16
Jidda, 44, 45, 54
Jim Murphy's midway, 125
Johnson, Bill and Dale, 152
Johnson, Charlene & Dickie, 154
Johnson, Jody, 154
Johnson, Rickie, 154
Jones, Braxton, 148
Jones, Maj. Nelson and Mary
    Ellen, 48, 116
Jones, Mary, 149, 191
July 25, 1969, 70
July 30, 1969, 71
June 15, 1969, 67
June 1973 Scout Citation, 94
June 30, 1978 Retired, 105
June 30, 1982, 122
Jungle Colonel, 137
Junior, 118, 120, 124, 127

K

Kailua, 50
Kalchik, Spc. Albion (Al), 163,
    165, 167, 168, 170, 174, 175
Kansas, 49
Kappa Alpha, 24
Katchie, Jim and Pat, 148
Kauai, 69
Kavoric, Maj.), 30
Keesler Airfield, 16
Kendall, Maj. Gen., 104
Kennedy Space Center, 104
kerosene lamps, 2
kerosene stove, 2
Key West, 48
King Company, 30, 31
King of Jordan, 46
King Saud, 45
King, Captain Wayne, 151
Kirkland, Ellis, 151
Knutsen, 1st Lt., 165
Koch, Brig. Gen. Robert, 88
Korea, 25, 27, 28, 30, 31
Korean War, 25
KP (kitchen police), 18, 20, 91
Kuwait, 179

L

Ladies Home Journal, 5
Lai Khe, 54, 55, 59, 60, 61, 69,
    70, 85, 86, 165, 166, 175
Lake George, 109, 152
Lake Kerr, 140, 142
Lambert, Kevin (LTC), 180
Landin, Luis, 146
lane grader, 40
Lane, Don, 144, 145, 166
Laos, 72
Leach, James, Colonel, 70, 74,
    80
leapfrog, 65

Ledoux, Barry and Portia, 151
Lee, Dennis, 132
Legion of Merit, 86, 106
Leslie, Harold, 134
Letterman Army Hospital, 171
Liberty Magazine, 5
Libya, 44
Lieutenant Colonel (rank), 50
Life Scout, 6
Little Havana, 5
Little Lake Kerr, 142
Little League, 53
Little, Desmond, 23
Lopes, David, 153
Lopes, Joseph and Engrid, 153
Love Company, 28
Lucius, Frank M., 151
Ludlow, Pfc. Douglas J., 144, 145, 192
Lyons, Gene, 120, 127
Lysik, Marie, 13

M

MacDill Air Force Base, 137
MacDill Army Airfield, 15
Mackedanz' story, 172–75
Mackedanz, Spc. Ron ('Mack'), 144, 158, 159, 163, 165, 167, 168, 170, 175, 176, 192
Madrid, 44
Maguire, T. L., M.D., 1
Major (rank), 48, 49
Mandrel, Louise, 127
Mann, Charles, 152
Mann, Herbert and Gracy, 152
March 25, 1953, 31
March 9, 2012, 192
Marchman, Fred K., 11, 23
Marino, Sam, 127
Martin, Brig. Gen. David C., 86, 93

Maryland State Fair, 117
Massey, Amber, 148
Massey, Joe and Jonie, 148
Massey, Spc., 167, 170, 171
Matheson, Maj. Gen., 95
May 22, 1978, 105
McArthur, General, 21
McClure, Col. Joseph, 99
McClure, JerriAnne, 103
McDonald, Allison, 153
McDonald, Skip, 153
McEldridge, Mel, 175
McElreath, Spc. Melvin, 166, 168, 170
McHaffey, Maxie and Jackie, 151
McHenry, Herbert, 144, 145, 166
McMillan, Jack, 113
Medal of Honor, 54, 58, 86, 205
Melin, Master Sgt. Norman, 153
Melin, Susan, 153
Merrin, Joe, 118
Merritt Island, 98
Methodist Church, 13, 33, 34, 43, 46, 52, 109
Metten, Barbara, 100
Meunier, Paul and Juanita, 152
Meyer, Christy, 117
Miami, 4, 5, 10
Miles, J. Albert (Jake) Jr., 134
military history teacher, 36
Miller, Reverend, 152
Milloy, Maj. Gen. Albert E., 48, 86, 192, 223
Minnis, Lee and Jo, 89
Mission Accomplished, 177
Model "A" Ford, 13
model airplanes, 5
Mohler, Lt. Col. Robert L., 101
Monterey, 41, 202
Moore, Frank, 125
Moore, Lonnie, 146

Morgan, "Sucky", 8
Morgan, "DoDo", 8
Morgan, "Panky", 8
Morgan, "Rat", 8
Morris, Leslie, 111
mosquito hordes, 14
Mount Fuji, 21
Mullins, Marvin, 151
Murphy, Jim, 120

N

Nagasaki, 18
NASA, 98
Nashville, 126
National Communications
    Security course, 91
NDPs, 58, 70
Needham, William Patterson
    ("Pat"), 149
neighbors at the farm, 4
Neuburn, Cindy, 149
Neuburn, Gator, 149
New Orleans, 142
New Port Richey, 11, 12, 13, 14,
    23, 24, 43
Newsome, Joe E., 134
Niagara Falls, 35
Nickolson, Dave, 116
night defensive positions (NDPs,
    58
Nixon, Pres. Richard M., 71
Norfleet, Henri Ellen, 13
November 14, 2006, 154
November 20, 1955, 33
Nuckols family, 7
Nuckols, C.B., 8, 24, 34, 189

O

Oahu, 49, 50, 69
Ocala National Forest, 109, 147
Ocklawaha River, 147

October 25, 1958, 39
Ollie, 10, 12
Olson, Capt. Robert, 69, 72, 77,
    144, 176, 177
Operation Kentucky Cougar, 74,
    84, 86, 167
Operation Overlord, 15
Orange Blossom Special, 10, 150
orange crate furniture, 36
orchids, 147
outhouse amenities, 2

P

P-40/P-51 aircraft, 23
Pacific fog, 41
Pacific Ocean, 41
parachute riggers, 45
Paratrooper badge, 38
Parke, Helen, 132
Parke, Roy, 119, 132
Parke, Roy & Parkesdale, 191
Parker family, 7
Parker, Robert, 52
Parkesdale Farm Market, 191
Parrish, Wayne, 146
Partin, Mr. (principal), 25
Pathfinder badge, 38
Patrick Air Force Base, 98
Patterson, Dona, 149
Pearl Harbor, 12, 15, 50, 152
Peggy's first flight, 35
Peggy's first snow, 35
Pentagon, 88, 91, 94, 143
people-movers, 118, 119
Perabo, Lt. George, 75, 145, 166
Persian Gulf, 44, 46
Peters, Willis, 111
Phillips, Mr. (Ampro), 134
Phoenix 1945, 20
Phoenix 2005, 145
Phuoc Long Province, 67

Phuoc Vinh, 59, 62, 66, 72
pickin' and strummin', 150
picking fruit, 13
pinning the Eagles, 94
pitcher pump, 1
Plant City, 1, 3, 4, 5, 7, 8, 27, 33, 34, 42, 43, 47, 52, 69, 88, 89, 105, 106, 109, 114, 117, 137, 139, 140, 142
Plant City Boy Scouts, 8
Plant City Lions Club, 3, 115
Plant City native, 138
platform instructor, 40
pneumonia, 16
Pollack, Jim and Dotty, 52
Pollock, Dotty, 34
Pontiac hardtop, 35, 41
Poris, Cliff, 146
Portugal, 44
Pospisil, Col. Joseph L., 99
Presidio of San Francisco, 171
Promotion Board, 105
promotion to Colonel, 94
pumping gasoline, 13
Punahou School, 50
Purchet, Col. Mickey, 102, 191

Q

Quan Loi, 54, 55, 56, 57, 58, 59, 70, 72, 74, 160

R

Rabourn, Master Sergeant Stephen, 83, 84, 92, 93, 144
Ramsdell family, 7
Randall, Brig. Gen. James D., 100, 102, 105, 106
Ranger Tab, 39
REACHING AN LOC, 159
Readiness Region IV, 104
Reconnaissance in Force), 69

Red Sea, 44
Redman, James L., 134
Reis, Reggie, 152
Reno, 142, 143, 144, 145, 176
Renshaw, Pvt. Mike, 146, 165
Retired Officers Assn, 137
retirement, 179
retirement date, 137
reunions, 142, 143, 144, 168, 169, 176, 180, 185
reunited, 88
Rickenbacker, Eddie, x, 17
Ritter, Clay and Betty Ann, 89
River Jordan, 46
Roach, Freddy, 131
Roberts, Maj. Gen. Elvy B., 74, 75, 223
Rogers, 1st Sgt Harold, 151
Rogers, Charles C., Lt. Col., 57
Roig, Jack and Dena, 153
Rome plow, 62, 65, 66
Rome plow operation, 72
Rome, Ralph, 166
Roosevelt, Pres. Franklin, 15
Rosenberg, Charlotte, 3, 115, 135
ROTC, 24, 25, 31, 103, 106, 155, 206
ROTC instructor, 33
Royal Saudi Arabian Airborne Battalion, 45
RPGs, 64
RPGs-a *zillion*, 80
Rumalla, Dr. Ashwin, 154
Russian NVA advisor, 93
Ruzzi, Lt. Col., 45

S

S-2 (intelligence officer), 81
Saigon, 51, 88
Salt Springs, 109, 137, 142
Salt Springs' People, 147–54

Sanders Street, 7
Sansone Park, 5
Sansone, Mike, 5
Sarasota, 27, 101
Satellite Beach, 103
Saturday Evening Post, 5
Saudi Arabia, 44
Saudi dialect, 42
saxophone, 7, 10
Schoenwald, Bob, 146
school band, 7
Scott Army Airfield, 18, 20
Scott, Harry and Ora, 4
Scruggs, Bill, 25
scuba diving, 45
Seiler, T.C. & Teddy, 150
Seiler, Walt, 150
Sell Rite Grocery Store, 10
selling magazines, 5
September 1, 1981, 116
September 11, 2001, 142
September 25, 1951, 27
Setting the Stage, 130
Shands Hospital, 154
Showa, Japan, 21
shrapnel wound, 83
Shuffstall, Lt. Col., 60
SICR, 51
Siegel, Spc., 165
Sikes, Gene, 52, 53
Sikes, Margaret, 34, 52
Silver Star Awards, 192
Simpson, Kevin, 148
Singapore, 51
Skillin, Gene, 154
Smith family, 7
Smith, B.M. (Mac), 134
Smith, Brig. Gen. Albert H., 60, 63, 64
Smith, Caroline, 156
Smith, Lt. Col. James, 183, 184
Smith, Mac, 7, 189

Smith, Mac and Cookie, 52
Smith, Maurice and Joan, 156
Smith, Patrick, 7
Snow, Panky, 116
snowbirds, 149
Snowden, J. L., 148
Snowden, Jarrett, 148
Snowden, Michele, 148
soda jerk, 13
some gave all, 85
Song Be, 59, 60, 62, 66, 67, 69
Spann family, 7
Sparkman, Amos L., 34, 46
Sparkman, Mom and Dad, 37, 40, 42, 43, 52, 69, 88
Sparkman, Mrs. Josephine, 34
Sparkman, Peggy Ann, 27, 188
Sparkman, Perry, 34, 109
Sparkman, Virginia, 34
Special Forces, 95
Square Meal Cafe, 148
St. Johns River, 109
St. Louis 1945, 18, 20
St. Louis 2007, 145
stage manager, 120
Standing Down, 105
Star Scout, 8
Starke, Florida, 26
State Department course, 44
Sterling, David, 146
stock market crash, 2
Storrs, Connecticut, 35
StraightShooters Band, 150
Strawberry Festival, 114, 115, 116
Strawberry Festival 1930, 3, 115
Strawberry Festival Directors, 133
Strawberry Queen, 3
strawberry shortcake, 128
Stuff & Such, 151
Styrofoam china, 36

sugar bowl, 36
Sullivan, Pat, 146
Sunbakken, Dale T., 146
Swamp, 106
Swartsel, Dale, 14, 24, 34
Swartsel, Eddy, 14, 24
Swindle, Ed and Myrtle Lou, 52

T

Talbott, Maj. Gen. Orwin C., 54,
  56, 60, 70, 71, 85, 223
talent agent, 126
Tampa, 4, 13, 101
Tampa Tribune, 13
Tan Son Nhut Air Base, 54, 88
Tarpon Springs, 23
Task Force (TF), 65
Teakwood Place, 109
Terrace Drive (the farm), 1
Terre Rouge, 59
Tever Street, 1, 4
Thailand, 51
the "Creek", 45
the "Swamp", 106
The Forest, 147
The Wall, 190
Thompson, Gil, 146
Throckmorton, Maj. Gen., 48
thump gun, 174
Thunder Road, 54, 63, 70, 72
Tillis, Mel, 151
Tokubo, Rod, 146
Tokyo, 21, 31
Tomlin Junior High, 7, 109
Townsend, Azalee, 13
tracks (APCs), 60
Training Aids Department, 37
Trinkle, James, 128
Tripler Army Hospital, 40
Truman, Pres. Harry S., 17
Tucker family, 7

turncoats, 61

U

U. Connecticut at Waterbury, 76
U.S. Army Air Corps boys, 44
Underwood, John, 140
University of Connecticut, 33, 36
University of Florida, 24, 106,
  149, 154
University of Manchester, 156
USS Missouri, 18

V

VA loan, 89
VE Day May 8, 1945, 17
Vermont, 116
Verner, Dr. & Mrs. John, 134
Verner, Mr. & Mrs. Edward, 134
Vernon, William (Billy), 134
Veterans Administration, 144
VFW Post, 151
Victory Gardens, 63
Videl, Carlos, 128
Viet Cong, 51, 61, 64, 172, 206
volunteer fireman, 13

W

Walden Lake, 105
Walden, Charlotte, 106
Walden, David, 34, 52
Walden, David & Charlotte, 52
Walden, Don & Family, 7
Wallace, Ed, 146
Waller family, 4, 7
Walters, Viola, 13
Ware, Maj. Gen. Keith L., 54,
  223
Warm Springs, Georgia, 15
Washington *on fire*, 90
Washington, D.C., 44, 88, 190

Washington, D.C. 2006, 145
Washington, George, 76
washtub, 2
Waterbury, 33, 35, 36
Waters, Col. and Olivia, 99
Watertown, 33, 35
Watson Clinic, 110
Watson, Allen, 10
Watson, Alma (Cassels), 1
Watson, Clyde, 10
Watson, George, 10
Watson, Hoyt, 10
Watson, Jewell (Barrett), 10
Watson, Maxie, 10
Watson, Olivet, 10, 12
Watson, Pearl (Shelton), 10
Watson, Roy, 10
Watson, Ruth, 10
wedding, 33
weekend warriors, 100
Wessling, Bill, 151
white shark, 45
Whitehead, Mary Evelyn, 34
Whitston, Col. David, 106

Who won the war of Yankee
    aggression?, 36
Wildwood, 8–11
Wilson, Gail, 190
Wilson, Joe, 45, 49, 54
Winn family, 7
Winslow, Don and Lois, 152
Wolff, Brig. Gen. Herbert E., 81
Woodrow Wilson Elementary
    School, 3, 4
woodworking shop, 112
Wright family, 4
wringer washing machine, 36

Y

Yalu River, 30
Yellow River, 39
Yokohama, Japan, 20, 27, 28

Z

zillion RPGs, 80
Zimmerman, Robert C., 11, 23

I AM AN AMERICAN SOLDIER

I am a warrior and a member of a team.
I serve the people of the United States,
and live the Army Values.
I will always place the mission first.

I will never accept defeat.
I will never quit.
I will never leave a fallen comrade.

I am disciplined, physically and mentally tough,
trained and proficient in my warrior tasks and drills.
I always maintain my arms, my equipment and myself.
I am an expert and I am a professional.
I stand ready to deploy, engage, and destroy the enemies
of the United States of America in close combat.
I am a guardian of freedom
and the American way of life.

I AM AN AMERICAN SOLDIER

Lt. Col. Kenneth G. Cassels
during service in Vietnam

Simplified map of southern end of South Vietnam
shows "fish hook" region and other areas
mentioned by the author

Maj. Gen. Orwin C. Talbott
BRO Division Commander 1968-69
Became commander, Fort Benning,
Georgia 1969

Maj. Gen. Albert E. Milloy
Division Commander 1969-1970
Brought the division back to
Fort Riley, Kansas 1970

Maj. Gen. Keith L. Ware
Medal of Honor from Italy 1945
Killed in action in 1968
near Quan Loi, Vietnam

Maj. Gen. Elvy B. Roberts
Saw him only once on 10 Aug. 1969.
He was the 1st Cavalry Division
commander in 1969
Operation Kentucky Cougar

Lt. Col. Charles Calvin Rogers
a true hero and a Medal of Honor winner
Ken Cassels was with Charlie in 1968, the night before
Charlie won the Medal of Honor for his actions at
Quan Loi, Vietnam, near the Cambodian border
Charlie was later promoted to the rank of Major General

fletchettes (circa WWI)
*Charlie Rogers, Medal of Honor
recipient, fired a lot of these
fletchettes against the enemy
to save a fire base*

Army   **Navy**   **Air Force**

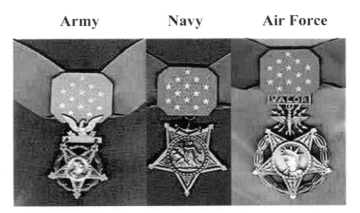

Present-Day Medals of Honor by Branch of Service

Purple Heart Medal
*Ken Cassels received the Purple Heart
for wounds received 5 September 1969
in action against the 273rd NVA Regiment*

*Note: Most of the photos on the following pages are
presented through the courtesy of Plant City Photo Archives*

*1985 Interview with Reporter
at Strawberry Festival*

Manager Emeritus 1996

Roy and Helen Parke 1983
Photo courtesy of Plant City Photo Archives

One of the Festival buildings
built by the WPA about 1938

Charlotte Rosenberg
Queen of the first Strawberry Festival (1930)
Ken Cassels attended her "coronation"
Photo courtesy of Plant City Photo Archives

March 1939
Children Waiting for a Festival Ride in Plant City, Florida
Photo Credit: Office of War Information
(*note the bare feet*)

Buddy Blain and C. B. Nuckols, Jr.
U.S. Navy Pharmacists Mates, Third Class
Buddy and C.B, were first cousins who joined the
U.S. Navy in 1945 and were discharged in 1947
Both were Eagle Scouts from Plant City
Photo courtesy of Plant City Photo Archives

Fred K. Marchman
Marguerite's Husband
Served his nation during WWII
and attained rank of Captain
Was a math teacher at Gulf High School
in New Port Richey, Florida

Bygone Days (circa 1959)
This was once a Plant City landmark
note the prices of the time
Photo courtesy of Plant City Photo Archives

Plant City (circa 1953)
corner of Collins and Reynolds Streets - the heart of town
Photo courtesy of Plant City Photo Archives

Reynolds Street in Plant City in Another Era
postcard by the E.C. Kropp Co., Milwaukee (circa approx. 1920)
Photo courtesy of Plant City Photo Archives

Orange Blossom Special

*The first diesel powered
passenger train in
the Southeast arrives
in Plant City
about December 1938*

State Archives of Florida
Florida Memory

Review

"*Duty–Honor–Country*" expresses ideals to live by in any age or generation, but they're vitally important to those on the front lines fighting for their lives and their country. With values he learned in the small town where he was born and from his experiences in scouting, the author lived a full life and traveled all over the world in service of his country. As he wrote this book, he discovered that few people knew what happened in the area of Vietnam where he served, especially from the viewpoint of those who were there.

Dry details from military reports do not vividly portray the life and death struggles of men fighting to survive the battles they were engaged in "on the ground" alongside their friends. They cannot show the courage and resourcefulness of those men, and they do not reflect their daring and heroism as they attempted to save themselves and their buddies against seemingly impossible odds. So, in writing this book, Col. Cassels has added personal accounts of some of the men who lived through those events in the fall of 1969 with him in a tribute to those who fought, and those who fell.

From "Jungle Colonel" to "Festival General," he left military service after more than 32 years. He taught exceptional students for a short time before becoming manager of the Strawberry Festival in late 1981. For 14 years he oversaw a vast expansion of the festival grounds and facilities. His contacts with the most famous country music artists of the day and his success in bringing their talent to the small-town festival helped make it the nationally famous attraction it still is today, in that same small town where he was born.

The basic traditions of the Boy Scouts of America influenced him throughout his life, helped build his core values and contributed to the heritage of his birthplace. An Eagle Scout, he never forgot the twelve points of the Scout Law, that scouts should be: *Trustworthy, Loyal, Helpful, Friendly, Courteous, Kind, Obedient, Cheerful, Thrifty, Brave, Clean, and Reverent,* has lived the Scout Motto of "*Be Prepared,*" and has kept the Scout Oath: *On my honor, I will do my best to do my duty to God and my country, and to obey the Scout law; to help other people at all times; to keep myself physically strong, mentally awake, and morally straight.*